CHRISTIAN SEXUALITY

 *Normative and Pastoral Principles*

Edited by
Russell E. Saltzman

CHRISTIAN SEXUALITY

Normative and Pastoral Principles

The Papers from the American Lutheran Publicity Bureau Conference

Held at Ruskin Heights Lutheran Church

Kansas City, Missouri

Edited by
Russell E. Saltzman

Kirk House Publishers
Minneapolis, Minnesota

ALPB Books
Delhi, New York

Christian Sexuality
Normative and Pastoral Principles
Edited by Russell E. Saltzman

Library of Congress Cataloging-in-Publication data
American Lutheran Publicity Bureau. Conference (2002 : Ruskin Heights Lutheran Church, Kansas City, Mo.)
    Christian sexuality : normative and pastoral principles : the papers from the American Lutheran Publicity Bureau Conference, held at Ruskin Heights Lutheran Church, Kansas City, Missouri / edited by Russell E. Saltzman.
       p. cm.
    Includes bibliographical references.
    ISBN: 1-886513-56-2 (perfect bound : alk. paper)
    1. Homosexuality--Religious aspects --Lutheran Church. 2. Pastoral theology. I. Saltzman, Russell E. II. Title.

BX8074.H65A47 2002
241'.66--dc22
                                    2003061889

Kirk House Publishers • PO Box 390759 • Minneapolis, MN 55439
American Lutheran Publicity Bureau • PO Box 327, Delhi, NY 13753
Printed and bound in the United States of America

 CONTENTS

 Introduction

There is no issue facing the Evangelical Lutheran Church in America (ELCA) more disvisive than the question of homosexual ordination and the blessing of same-sex unions.

I attended the 2001 ELCA churchwide assembly. Pending before the assembly was a resolution to simply change the present ELCA prohibition against ordaining non-celibate homosexuals, to take effect 2003. While a last-minute amendment changed the character of the resolution from one of mandate to merely study, it was my distinct impression the resolution could very well have been adopted. Other informed observers will dispute my assessment of the assembly's mood, yet they will concede that "pro-gay" issues, as they have arisen at churchwide assemblies, have gained ever-increasing support in the years following formation of the ELCA. In either case, it did become clear to me in a way as never before that ordination of non-celibate homosexuals (and the consequent blessing of same-sex unions) was an idea whose time was rapidly approaching ... unless something happened to alter the shape of the conversation.

Thus was born the idea of a conference on Christian sexuality. We are hearing quite enough about "human sexuality." Perhaps it was time to examine sexuality strictly from a Christian perspective. In short, I wanted a conference that would vigorously and with pastoral sternness unapolegitically set forth the traditional teaching of the Christian church; to set it forth in clear terms and again restate the classical sexual ethic that has marked the teaching of the Christian church from its earliest centuries.

That conference was held in October 2002 at Ruskin Heights Lutheran Church in Kansas City, Missouri, under the sponsorship of the American Lutheran Publicity Bureau (www.alpb.org), publishers of *Lutheran Forum* and *Forum Letter*, and carried endorsements from the

WordAlone Network and the Fellowship of Confessional Lutherans. Some 300 pastors and laity from around the nation heard a principled defense of the traditonal sexual ethic. The papers from the conference comprise the material in this volume, along with the *Statement of Pastoral Concern and Conviction* (which has been signed by over 1,700 pastors, lay people, church councils and congregations since it was issued).

What I did not want was an "anti-gay rally," and it was not. The conference was exactly as I envisioned—a pastoral theological conference to uphold the church's sexual ethic. An extremely sensitive topic was discussed with great sensitivity and—I believe—with honest pastoral concern.

I view this struggle as a theological struggle for the gospel. As I have told gay acquaintances, I am not your enemy but I am opposed to your theology. And I will fight it.

But that does not in the least diminish my pastoral sensitivity to their spiritual need, their quest for the love of God, their devout faith. I would like—for several personal reasons—to find a biblical hermeneutic and a doctrinal theology of creation that admits homosexuality. I hold in memory my college roommate who became an Episcopal priest. A homosexual African-American, he was serving as a curate in Cincinnati the year I entered seminary in Columbus, Ohio. My first sermon as a seminarian was in his parish. He died of AIDS eight years ago, and I grieve for him yet. As much for him as for other gays I know, I would like to just say "yes."

But I am convinced that "gay theology" is anti-gospel. Gay theology intends to alter our view of Scripture, our doctrine of creation, our theology of marriage, and our doctrine of the nature of sin—all of which exist in service to our understanding of the gospel. What is proposed by gay theology is nothing less than a different doctrine of Scripture, a different doctrine of creation, a different theology of marrage, a different doctrine of sin.

The essays here challenge and critique the theology of homosexuality. Robert Benne explains how the ELCA came to this moment and what homosexuality means to marriage. James Nestingen examines the subject in light of the law/gospel conversation in which Lutherans must engage.

Thomas A. Skrenes honestly asks about his ministry as a bishop, if the ELCA changes its current practice. My essay speaks about the accomodation granted to divorced pastors, and why it is not analogous to non-celibate gay pastors. Amy C. Schifrin alerts readers to the often underestimated force of ritual, asking especially what are same-sex blessings actually ritualizing; she also addresses the question of why women's ordination is different than the ordination of gays.

Phillip Max Johnson's pastoral meditation challenges us to understand the interplay between our natural bodies and our spiritual destiny, and what this says to both homosexuals and herterosexuals. Merton Strommen, a pastor, psychologist and founder of the Augsburg Youth Institute, describes the forces at work in our culture to normalize homosexuality, and the impact this is having on American youth.

Two non-Lutherans also appear. Robert A. J. Gagnon, a distinguished Presbyterian biblical scholar, takes us back to the Bible. His is a very detailed but worthy explanation of what the Bible does say. Jay Scott Newman, a Catholic priest, offers a blunt ecumenical warning to Lutherans should the ELCA proceed with approval of non-celbiate homosexual ordinations.

The sexual irregularities attributed to the homosexual are but a reflection of the sexual irregularities among the heterosexual—serial marriage, live-ins, child abuse, the growth of pornography and the other social troubles that confront our culture—and you will hear this clearly in the essays. To this point, however, the question isn't whether the church may tolerate ordained and sexually active homosexuals in particular (I do not believe it can), but why the church is so tolerant of sexual irregularity in general? Yet granting grave irregularities among heterosexuals, and they are grave, there remains a crucial difference. No one regards the sexual social disorder of heterosexuals as good. Each example of sexual irregularity, whether it springs from homosexual or heterosexual inclination, remains a manifestation of that sin to which we all are captive.

But to adopt benign policies toward gay unions and gay ordination, we must jettison all of what we know of the Judaic/Christian sexual ethic. We must revise our understanding of creation, the Fall, original sin, and overturn each in favor of something altogether different. What we are presented with is the challenge, in St. Paul's phrase, of "a different gospel."

Russell E. Saltzman, pastor
Ruskin Heights Lutheran Church
Kansas City, Missouri
Editor, *Forum Letter*

✵ Chapter One

The Limits of Tolerance:
Homosexuality and the ELCA's LPD (Liberal Protestant Drift)

By Robert Benne

The Present Situation

"Not with a bang, but a whimper" describes how mainstream Protestantism seems to be ending. True, the various mainstream denominations still exist at the beginning of the 21st century, but I suspect there won't be much left of them by mid-century. They may be gathered into one "Protestant Church of America," but the mergers will take place out of weakness rather than strength. They simply don't have enough clarity about, confidence in, and zeal for the gospel — the full Trinitarian faith — to replenish their own membership from within or to gain enough converts from without.

The societal pressures on religious traditions to accommodate to a highly individualistic, postmodern culture will be enormous. As H. Richard Niebuhr warned many years ago in his *Christ and Culture*, those traditions who once maintained a strong tension between the transcendent Christ and the immanent culture, will find themselves slowly moving toward the Christ of Culture camp. Only the strongest traditions will survive with their identity intact as our culture exerts pervasive pressure to accommodate to it. The others, such as the various liberal Protestant denominations, will decline and probably merge.

For a long time we Lutherans believed we were different from the Protestant mainstream. Quite a few non-Lutheran scholars and national commentators thought so too. We had a strong confessional tradition, a robust heritage and practice of theological reflection, a liturgical tradition, and a strong sense of identity and loyalty, partly due to our ethnic character. Lutherans had a great affection for their churches. Throughout the postwar 40s, 50s, and 60s we grew in numbers and vitality.

But the scene is very different today. We no longer have the confidence that we are different, and therefore have a strong reason for continued existence. A number of our brightest lights have gone to other more stable traditions. Our confessional tradition is fairly irrelevant, our theological reflection has broken into a thousand voices, our sense of loyalty and identity is weak, and we are aging and declining. We congratulate ourselves in finally joining our social betters — the Episcopalians, Presbyterians, and the United Church of Christ — in their loss of clarity, confidence, and zeal for the gospel. The combined "Protestant Church in America" looks like it is just around the corner.

Mainstream merger

How do we account for this merger into the mainstream? As I have suggested, a great deal of it is due to the enormous pressures for accommodation with culture. But we have given additional punch to those pressures by our own self-conscious actions. We have aided the deconstruction of the Lutheran tradition by adopting the ideas and practices of elite, liberal culture. Foremost, among them is our adoption of a left-wing scheme of representation that ensured "inclusivity" by quotas. "Inclusivity is the central theme of the Evangelical Lutheran Church in American (ELCA). However, "inclusivity" is not catholicity, which would mean a concerted effort to evangelize many kinds and types of people, and invite them to work their way into the leadership of the church. Who would not be for such catholicity?

Instead, inclusivity means a scheme of representation that makes all committees, boards, councils, and faculties subject to the percentages of minorities and designated oppressed groups we would *like* to have in the church, not the ones we have in the church. It aims at equality of results, measured by those percentages. It is radically skeptical in that it assumes that racist, sexist Lutherans simply will not do the right thing in electing or appointing people, radically condescending in assuming that minorities cannot earn leadership positions on their own merits, and radically optimistic in the conviction that the people turned up by the quota system will be Lutherans who are deeply embedded in the vision and ethos of Lutheranism. The architects of this scheme wanted to diminish the authority of the white males who carried the theological DNA of Lutheranism and open it up for many other voices. Inclusivity and diversity were meant to invade theology as well as representation, and they have.

This virus has been deeply driven into the fabric of the ELCA. It has turned the church into a chaotic cacophony of voices, none of them particularly authoritative. We have become a model of interest group liberalism. Theologians are viewed as one interest group among many. The only theology honored is one that exalts a gospel without law. Since we have cut ourselves off from the authority of past churches, the theological and moral traditions we have held to be authoritative are now reduced to same level as the many voices we have invited into the conversation. There is little orthodoxy to overthrow.

However, the effect of "inclusivity" has not been neutral, ideologically speaking. Theological revisionism and social and political liberalism characterize the official organs of the ELCA, partly because only revisionists and liberals accept the idea of quotas and can therefore be selected, and partly because "inclusivity" has not yet been expanded to include theological traditionalists and social and political conservatives.

One only has to look at the drift of Augsburg Fortress Publishers, *The Lutheran*, Women of the ELCA, Lutheran Office of Governmental Affairs, the ELCA Church Council, Church in Society, Global Mission Events, many of our seminaries, campus ministry on secular campuses, and our presiding bishop's recent statements to get an accurate picture of the liberal protestantizing of our church. The sacred topics of Protestant liberalism pervade our doings as much as, say, the Episcopalians. (To be fair, however, it is important to note that some attempts at re-centering several of these expressions of the church have been made, and we should encourage them.)

While this drift is irritating, if not alienating, it has been tolerated by most of us. After all, there are many great parishes and people within the ELCA. The Lutheran network provides a circle of Christian friends and institutions that are dear to me. We are still a Christian church. So we cope. So, I — like many others — have reluctantly tolerated the "LPD — Liberal Protestant Drift" of the ELCA.

Coming to the limits

But on these issues of sexuality we have come to the limits of toleration. (True tolerance, as I will argue later, does not mean limitless elasticity; it includes notions of endurance and forbearance. When certain limits are exceeded, tolerance cannot forbear or endure any longer.) I believe that the proposals to bless homosexual unions and ordain homosexuals in committed relationships strain the level of tolerance for orthodox Christians. Even the fact that the ELCA is taking those proposals seriously raises the level of our alienation from the ELCA. Can such settled Christian moral teachings really come under serious questioning? Can they actually be voted on in assemblies?

But were the ELCA to accept those proposals, their acceptance would do more than increase our alienation or strain our tolerance. Acceptance would raise the issue of *status confessionis* for many of us. Acceptance would constitute a frontal assault on the core meanings and values of the Christian faith. Acceptance would involve a denial of the basics of the Trinitarian faith, not just a difference of opinion. Acceptance would mean a rejection of the commandments of God. That cannot be tolerated.

There is a good deal of pessimism that the ELCA will accept those proposals, for all the reasons I have already enumerated. That pessimism is well founded. We have the memory of the ELCA's first incredible effort at making a statement on sexuality. It was a perfect product of the forces I described above. After the fall-out from that debacle, I was miraculously appointed to an ELCA task force to deliberate about how the ELCA might deliberate about sexuality issues. I found that I was the only one on the task force of about a dozen willing to speak for the traditional teaching on these matters. The general assumption of the vocal majority was that all the issues had been settled in their minds and it was time to enlighten the minions of darkness in the ELCA.

The host of materials and actions of many ELCA organs that have followed have reinforced the perception that the mind of the ELCA is indeed made up, all that remains is the *coup detat*. The new task force that has been appointed is pretty well stacked according to the ELCA "LPD." But we should not give up prematurely. A genuine theological dialogue in the task force and in the ELCA in general may well emerge as we draw nearer to 2005. We need to make our own contributions to that dialogue in the time we have left.

The argument for tradition

The Jewish and Christian traditions have been opposed to homosexual sexual relations, though not always in a punitive fashion. Their prohibitions follow from their belief that there is a divinely created structure to sexual life. Women and men are meant to complement each other. They "fit" together physically, emotionally, and spiritually. Male and female God created them, and they are meant to be as one within the bonds of marriage. In other words, there is *form* to the creation. Moral sexual relations are appropriate to form. This consideration rejects sexual activities between adults and children, between humans and animals, between family members, and between persons of the same sex. The Ten Commandments assume and order such a normative form.

This negative posture remains intact among the vast majority of Jewish and Christian traditions, despite strong attacks on it from some secular authorities in legal, medical, psychological, and social-scientific fields as well as challenges to it from a number of Christian scholars and Christian advocacy groups. Indeed, the challenges from within mainstream Christian denominations have been so sharp and relentless that they threaten to split them. The controversy is a very serious one, with both sides — the traditionalists and the revisionists — holding fiercely to their positions. A large group in the middle does not know what to think.

The gist of the revisionist argument contends that there really is no persisting, discernible sexual identity tied to the obvious differences in biological form. Traditional differences, they argue, are oppressive cultural definitions imposed by heterosexual males that have proven to be highly relative, both from culture to culture and from person to person within a culture. Thus, they counsel that love between persons be the sole criterion governing sexual relations. "All you need is love." The "appropriate to form" qualification should be dropped, at least as it pertains to homosexual relations. Homosexual relations are not disordered or imperfect, only different. There is less interest in dropping the "appropriate to form" qualification with regard to incest, pedophilia, and bestiality though it is difficult to see why those barriers should not also fall, given their argument.

Nevertheless, those responsible for Christian moral tradition are not convinced. Neither is this writer. The biblical position seems fairly clear and straightforward in spite of the efforts to relativize it through historical-critical studies. At least two of the Ten Commandments assume the heterosexual nature of the marriage bond, as do the creation stories in Genesis. The whole structure of the Bible is heterosexual; the revisionists bear this out by calling it "heterosexist." Church tradition is rather unequivocal. There is nothing in either the Bible or Christian teaching that can be retrieved to legitimate homosexual relations, as there were with the issues of slavery and women's leadership in the church. The revisionists are now even admitting that one cannot make a case for legitimating homosexual unions on the basis of the Bible or the tradition.

Besides the Bible and Christian tradition, human experience seems to suggest that sexual identity has deep roots in persisting biological form. The tendency of cultures to differentiate clearly between male and female sexual identities indicates a continuing bias toward complementary sexual identities and roles. They prize child-bearing and raising within stable unions of male and female.

There is scarcely any warrant, therefore, in abandoning the "appropriate to form" requirement; neither for Christians in general nor especially for the leadership of the church. Churches must confidently and clearly teach the normative Christian moral teaching on these matters that has been in place for thousands of years. Overturning the tradition's moral presumption against homosexual relations would take far more evidence against it than we have now.

Pastoral approaches

This does not mean, however, that the church cannot have a nuanced and compassionate pastoral approach to homosexuals. Without relaxing its affirmation of heterosexual sex within the marriage covenant, the church can strongly insist that the gospel is addressed to all sinners. Homosexual activity is not some especially heinous sin that cuts one off from God's grace. Consistent with this, inclusion within the church and its pastoral care should be insisted on.

As with all sin, though, forgiveness follows repentance and leads to efforts to follow God's will insofar as it is discerned by the church. The church should continue to call those who are homosexual by orientation — derived from either biological or environmental factors — to a "heroic" response. That is, they should be called to practice sexual abstinence, sublimating their sexual energies into other pursuits. The church has long honored such "heroic" responses for homosexual and heterosexual singles alike, and should continue to do so. Indeed, such a response should be the only one allowed for ordained clergy, who have vowed to exemplify the ideals of the church.

It would be naïve to argue that this can be the church's only response for lay Christians. In our present culture, some lay Christians who are homosexual by orientation will engage in sexual relations with members of their own sex. Some will act promiscuously but others will seek more stable unions. Many homosexuals will remain "in the closet" and participate incognito in church life, but others will insist that the church formally recognize their sexual identity and bless their unions. Gays and lesbians of all sorts of persuasion are present in our churches, and there seems to be widespread confusion about the church's proper pastoral response to this fact. Given the normative teaching outlined above, what pastoral strategy toward homosexuals should be adopted by churches and Christian individuals?

Gracious tolerance

I would propose a strategy of *gracious tolerance*. By "gracious" I mean that the church—both clergy and lay—should greet all persons coming into the fellowship of the church with a warm welcome. After all, we are a company of forgiven sinners. Many homosexuals who prefer to keep their sexual identity private will accept this welcome and participate fully in the life of the church. Many who are in partnered relationships may also wish to keep the sexual nature of their friendships hidden or unclear. As long as such persons do not openly violate or flaunt the normative teachings of the church, they should also be greeted and accepted graciously. The church can even affirm the rich elements of friendship in their ongoing relationship, though not its sexual elements. The latter need not be revealed or probed. The church does not probe others who do not live up to the moral ideals of the church. Kindliness, inclusion, and support would be the order of the day in these cases, as it is for all the church's members. Repentance, forgiveness, and amendment of life should be left for homosexuals to work out privately, as is the case for other persons who struggle with the moral demands of the Christian life.

For those who are struggling with sexual identity in their lives, "graciousness" would mean first of all an effort to help them sort out who they are and who they wish to become. Though some homosexuals seem irretrievably caught in their same-sex desires, many young people are simply confused about their sexual identities. It is gracious to the latter to help them move toward heterosexual desires so that they can grow in that direction in their prospective sexual relationships. For those persons who have inclinations toward same-sex desires but who want to move toward a heterosexual identity, various therapies may be helpful. For both these kinds of persons, it is particularly important that the public teaching of the church affirm heterosexual norms.

For those who seem "fixed" in their orientation, it is consistent with our argument above to counsel abstinence. Like other singles, homosexuals are called to refrain from sexual relations. In cases in which abstinence is not being observed, it is gracious privately and tentatively to encourage sexual fidelity within committed friendships. Such an arrangement is far better than the dangerous promiscuity practiced by a significant portion of the homosexual subculture. From a Christian point of view, it is the lesser of evils. But their sexual relations are still disordered and imperfect, even though other elements in their friendship are admirable. It is important continually to hold up the Christian ideal before such homosexual pairs. Perhaps in time they can work toward celibate friendships. Perhaps some may wish to engage in reparative therapy. This gradual process assumes a strong pastoral commitment to such pairs. Without that the pastoral counsel will sound simply as judgmental hectoring.

It would be disastrously wrong publicly to bless such arrangements. It would send too many wrong messages to the church. To those who regard homosexual relations as sinful, it would signal that the church blesses sin. To those who are struggling with their own sexual identity, it would put an imprimatur on desires and activities they need to resist. Opposition to public blessing reminds us that there are limits to the church's graciousness. Those limits have to do with tolerance, the second word in our phrase *gracious tolerance*.

Forbearance and endurance

Tolerance does not mean that anything goes, as our permissive culture tends to view it. Tolerance, while it suggests a liberal and open-minded attitude toward persons whose beliefs and actions are different from one's own, also denotes forbearance and endurance. Tolerance, therefore, has its limits. (A bridge, for example, tolerates a certain tonnage but no more.) We tolerate — that is, we forebear and endure — beliefs and actions that diverge from our own. However, if certain beliefs and actions violate our core convictions, we do not tolerate them. We oppose them and act against them. And properly so; personal integrity and courage are at stake. On the other hand, our level of tolerance is more elastic with regards to beliefs and actions that go counter to our less central or peripheral values, such as our preferences, tastes, or opinions.

The church, like individuals, can tolerate all sorts of opinions and practices that involve peripheral matters. It can allow a great deal of latitude on how Christians should apply Christian moral teachings to issues of public policy. It can tolerate a number of forms of worship and preaching. It can tolerate sharp disagreements about practical matters that, while important, are not essential to the core teaching and practices of the church. It can even tolerate many persons whose behavior is out of line with its teaching. Indeed, it can — and must — tolerate all of us sinners who fall short of what the commandments of God demand. In a sense we are all tolerated by the church.

However, the church is the Body of Christ, responsible for maintaining its apostolic witness. It is entrusted by its Lord with the gospel — the full-blown Trinitarian faith, as well as with the central practices that follow from it. Certainly the commandments are included in its moral core. Therefore, direct, public challenges in word and deed to its core convictions and practices simply cannot be tolerated. Challenges to the tradition's teaching on homosexuality are directed at that core.

This does not mean that those core convictions and practices cannot be discussed and debated. There must be a zone of freedom where persons can carry on spirited conversation on central issues that are puzzling or even offensive to them. The youth of the church must be allowed to ask questions about those key issues. Such a zone should be provided in the educational program of the church. At regional and national levels of the church there is room for such discussion. But the proliferation of opinions at that level should not confuse or qualify the normative teaching of the church in its preaching or catechesis. At the level of normative, official teaching and preaching, the church has a tradition to convey clearly and confidently. Official representatives of the church are obligated to preserve and convey that tradition until it is officially changed, and on core issues, that change can only come after decades of reflection, discussion, and prayer.

With regard to these sexuality issues, the church cannot tolerate significant "cultures of dissent" that publicly impugn the teaching of the church by contrary teaching and behavior. Permissiveness toward such dissenters makes the church appear hypocritical, ineffectual, or unwilling to hold dissenters accountable to its moral teachings. In recent years it has led to crises of sexual misconduct in both Protestantism and Catholicism.[1] Likewise, if it is to be one church, it cannot tolerate public repudiation of its teachings by individual congregations or synods. Nor can it tolerate a compromise in which both the traditional and the revisionist perspectives officially co-exist, for that means that the teaching of church has indeed changed; there is no normative perspective on these matters. The one church must maintain its unified, normative tradition in a disciplined fashion until it is changed.

Finally, the church cannot tolerate relentless and unceasing challenges to its normative teaching on sexuality. Such is the route to depletion and decrease. There has to be an agreement that its settled convictions cannot be challenged indefinitely. Once a church has re-affirmed its teaching, there has to be a decent interval of surcease from continued challenges.

Needing grace and renewal

Such, I believe are the normative and pastoral principles that should hold sway in the ELCA. Much has happened in recent decades to sensitize us to the plight of our Christian homosexual brothers and sisters. Those brothers and sisters have made us aware of the toll that harsh rejection in church and society has taken on them. Most Christians have come to the realization that we cannot treat them as modern day lepers whose whole being is denied. These brothers and sisters are persons who need grace and renewal like we are. They need Christian friendship. I hope that they can find some measure of graciousness in the approach I have outlined.

However, I simply cannot swallow hard and accept the revisionist claim that the church can publicly bless homosexual unions and allow homosexuals in partnered relationships to be pastors in the ELCA. The Bible, the Lutheran tradition, and the great Catholic and Orthodox traditions clearly come to quite different conclusions. The laity of the churches do too. In a recent survey by Barna Research, lay persons by a 2 to 1 ratio believe that homosexual relations are proscribed by the Bible. But about one fifth of them are now uncertain; they have been confused by the current debate. The ELCA clergy are another matter; I would guess that they tip in the revisionist direction.

Our success in preventing the ELCA from continuing on its disastrous "LPD" depends upon our capacity to awaken the laity and get them to project their voices. Thus, it is crucially important that the statement that comes out of this conference be made widely available to laity and clergy alike.[2] That awakening, demonstrating clearly that our arguments coincide with the Bible and the Lutheran tradition, can summon the church to continued fidelity to its historic teaching. For this we hope and pray.

Robert Benne is professor of religion at Roanoke College, Roanoke, Virginia, and is the director of its Center for Church and Society. He is the author of numerous books, including Ordinary Saints, *and his articles have appeared in* The Cresset, First Things, Lutheran Forum *and other publications.*

---

[1] Well-informed confidants tell me that this "culture of dissent" is already established in at least two seminaries. These confidants allege: one seminary has two pairs of faculty living in same-sex unions. Only a small minority of faculty object to this, and then not publicly. Homosexuals constitute at least one third of the student body at another. There is eager exploration of different sexual identities and partners, much to the shock of the heterosexual students, especially the married couples. Activist Christian homosexual organizations on campus are torn by conflict between a faction that wants to be held accountable to heterosexual standards of sexual fidelity and a faction that does not want to be bound by them. The irregularly ordained gay pastor of a nearby ELCA congrega-

tion confides that many Christian male homosexuals simply will not observe sexual fidelity in their unions. Should such dissent continue it is not hard to envision a situation in the ELCA similar to that in the American Catholic church, where both the vows of chastity and prohibitions against homosexual relations were flaunted with impunity by many priests. If the venerable institution of the celibate Catholic priesthood can be thus subverted, why not the institution of Christian marriage with its confining notions of sexual fidelity?

[2] A reference to the *Pastoral Statement of Conviction and Concern*. See appendix for the full text.

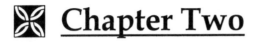 Chapter Two

Is There a Law?
The Lutheran Reformation and Homosexual Practice

By James A. Nestingen

The original Lutheran documents set up around two central themes — the justification of the godless and the vocations of everyday life. As Martin Luther wrote in *The Freedom of the Christian*, restored to relationship for which we were created by the death and resurrection of Christ Jesus and so set free from the powers of death and desolation, "the Christian is the perfectly free Lord of all, subject to none." At the same time, in Christ, the Christian is "...the perfectly dutiful servant of all, subject to all," called into the service set out by the day.

Taking the Catholic tradition

Convinced of the biblical priority of these themes for a church turned in on itself at the time of the Reformation, the original Lutherans did not attempt to build a complete new theological or ethical system. Instead, they took as their own the Catholic tradition of the church, attempting first of all to reorient its preaching and worship and then to correct points where they thought it had gone astray. As they re-thought the tradition, the Lutherans worked with distinctions they took to be required by their themes, such as the distinction between law and gospel, two kingdoms and others.

Because they approached things this way, there is no particularly Lutheran teaching on homosexual practice. Martin Luther, Philip Melanchthon and others who wrote, either unofficially or officially, clearly knew the standard biblical texts along with traditional Christian teachings. They were also well aware of violations, especially among an officially celibate clergy. While oftentimes critical of Roman Catholic views of sexuality, they accepted as a given, requiring little or no comment, the church's universal condemnation of homosexual practices. In fact, given their biblical way of thinking, the reformers might wonder how the church's endorsement of homosexual practice ever got to be an issue for ELCA consideration.

This said, the Lutheran heritage still has something to say in approaching issues of sexual ethics. Its voice can be heard in a couple of ways. One is to go through the Lutheran sources and collect the different points that relate to sexual matters, using the classic distinctions to think them through. The second is to look at a contemporary interpretation of social ethics that has been authoritative for American Lutherans and see how it might apply.

Beginning with justification by faith puts a strong priority on the forgiveness of sins in its spoken and sacramental form. As a gathering of sinners assembled by the Holy Spirit by and for the preaching of God's Word and the administration of the sacraments, the church exists to assure those caught up under the powers of the world as we know it — be they personal, social, private, public, corporate or cosmic — of the triune God's love in restoring the creation. The church is the church when it declares to sinners, sexual or otherwise, the promise of the gospel and so serves their coming into the relationships for which all were intended: faith, hope and love. Since the Trinity is ultimately the speaker of this word, the one who authorizes its declaration, it is complete, unconditional, and free. The only possible parallels are creation out of nothing or the resurrection of the dead.

Distinguishing law and gospel

One of the first consequences of this priority involves the law. Thus justification takes place "apart from the law," as the Apostle Paul says, or "without the law" (Galatians 2:15-21). Or to put it in the language of the Gospel of John, since Christ is "the way, the truth and the life," the law can't be (John 14:6, 1:17). But this raises an immediate question, in the New Testament itself, in the Lutheran sources and in disputes with alternative readings of the Christian faith: what about the law? There are moral requirements in Scripture, there are legal requirements in the state, and rules are everywhere! What are they for? Justification by faith requires a distinction between law and gospel, one of the key aspects of Lutheran thinking.

Luther answers the question as Paul did, correlating the law with sin. The gospel of God's love for sinners in Christ Jesus doesn't change —

it is the first and last word. But when the gospel promise is spoken, declaring the forgiveness of sins, deliverance and the resurrection, the law appears in an entirely different light. It gets reduced to terms, put in proportion, taken out of the determinative position to become a word as opposed to the Word.

Approached in this way, for the original Lutherans, the question of the law's purpose becomes a down-to-earth problem of description. What is the law for? The answer is not as much a theological definition as it is a description of what the law actually does do in human experience. While it can't make love, engender hope or create faith, the law is generally good at keeping order. It is not perfect, not by any means, but in roughly seven or eight cases, maybe even nine out of ten, the law brings enough restraint to keep things working the way they are supposed to work. In this capacity, the law restrains evil and can also point to the necessity of justice and peace in the household, in the community and in the larger world.

In the light of the gospel, another capacity of the law appears, one that appears in vague outlines apart from Christ Jesus. In the world as we now know it, the law has a way of turning on a person, focusing on the defining relationships to attack, expose, or above all to accuse. The occasion of the law's attack might be a moral problem; more commonly, it has something to do with a person's sense of standing in relation to the family, work, and the public or to God. In fact, when the law assaults in this way, it shows its characteristic power in this life. It has a way of compounding itself in a person's sense of self until it becomes virtually demonic, an ally of sin and death. As it has traditionally been put, the law works wrath.

Distinguishing law and gospel in this way, Luther repeatedly returned to preach and write on the Ten Commandments to show their place in the ordering of life. The commandments are scriptural, they are fundamental to the law of Israel, and they have had an important place in the Catholic tradition. But to Luther, their authority rests in the simple and direct way that they codify the fundamental relationships of everyday life. They formulate what is required of all people in the web of inter-dependence necessary to life.

Three commandments relate to sexual matters. In the traditional Catholic numbering, the Fourth says, "Honor your father and mother." It is assumed here that life is inherently familial. Children enter the world out of a relationship between a woman and a man. By the act of parenthood, mother and father assume responsibility for the child — nurturing, protecting and training until there is sufficient maturity for the child to leave home. If this responsibility is not shouldered, others will have to step in for the child. Delicate, complex and basic to the shape of a child's life, family relationships by their very nature demand honor — a combination of love, deference and respect flowing back and forth among parents and children. Though there are always exceptions, the quality of family relationships generally plays itself out for a life-time, for good or ill. As such, the commandment to honor is basic to the shape of life itself.

The explanation of the Sixth Commandment follows suit. The prohibition of adultery rejects sexual relations, defined as mutual genital activity, apart from marriage. But as Luther interprets the commandment, the negative assumes the positive — that "husband and wife love and honor one another." Again, the nature of the relationship demands such a cherishing, not only because life begins sexually but also because intimacy thrives best where love and honor prevail. Uniting sinners for a lifetime carries high risk; the prohibition of adultery protects the whole family relationship so that its positive dimensions can develop.

Eliminating the original biblical commandment against graven images, the Catholic tradition split the biblical Tenth Commandment against covetousness into two, the Ninth dealing with the house, the Tenth with a person's relationships. Luther follows the tradition, explaining both commandments in terms of the craftiness, tricks and enticements used by sinners to deprive others of what is rightfully theirs while still seeking to maintain a legal appearance.

While the numbering is the same, a difference between the Lutherans and the Catholic tradition shows up here. Following selected writings of St. Augustine, who summed up the theology of the early church and laid the basis for medieval Catholicism, the church had focused on desire itself and particularly sexual desire to locate the prime sin. So in the Catholicism Luther and the reformers knew, the traditional language of sin, including words like "concupiscence," insatiable desire, or "lust," was sexually charged. Inordinate desire breaks into disorder, turning people from the spiritual to the carnal, from the lofty concerns of the soul to the baser agendas of the flesh.

Luther and Philip Melanchthon, his colleague and friend, the final editor of the Augsburg Confession and another major influence in the Lutheran reformation, redefined the terms. As they saw it, the root or prime sin arises in the deeper regions of the human heart — the disordered loves of sexual longing grow out of the sinner's determination "...to be wise, to know good from evil" (Genesis 3:5), and so to avoid death. It is the desire to justify the self, to get control of the sources of life and bend them to personal purpose, to become my own project working out my own significance and value. In the medieval Catholic tradition the Lutherans knew, the prime sin was sexual; as the Lutherans saw it, the prime sin is religious, seeking the power and value of life in "creatures, saints and devils," as Luther put it. Finally, it is idolatry — the sin of the First Commandment.

Disordered sexual longing

This difference between the medieval Catholic tradition and the Lutherans plays itself out in relation to the Ninth and Tenth Commandments in general and matters of sexuality in particular. Because the root sin is disordered sexual longing, the medieval church sought to regulate desire and so to restore order by setting up structures in which the truly devout withdrew from sexual contact. Monks and nuns had for centuries taken vows of celibacy; in the 11th century, the same requirement was made of all the clergy. While marriage was honored as a sacrament, it was of a lesser order — the truly devout could only be so by renouncing sexual relations. Women in particular bore an onus, being held responsible for lust's continuing power.

The Lutherans went a different direction. Luther had had enough struggles with his own heart, and had spent enough time in the confessional listening to people's accounts of their personal battles, to know the limits of the law's power. It can regulate external behavior — like the plots and schemes of the covetous — but the powers at work in the human heart are more controlling than simple will power. Repressed in sinners, desire multiplies against itself, gaining a life of its own and so even greater dominance. In the process, covetousness becomes idolatry, exalting the object of its longings — whether thing or person — beyond human proportions, possessing the desirer like grim fate. Even if the heart can't be reached, the external act has to be restrained by law — for the sake of the one desiring, the safety of the desired and the well being of the community. Disordered sexual longings are not the prime sin, but sexuality is an aspect of life where the power of sin expresses itself and so demands regulation for everyone concerned.

At the same time, in proportion with all of the other aspects of human self-hood, sexuality is one of the great goods of creaturely life. With it, God gives the deep companionship of marital life. And through it, God continues to bestow life in the creation, using women and men as his "hands" or "channels" to create a future for the community and the earth itself. In this context, sexual desire reveals its goodness, bringing couples together to serve one another, God and the community.

Recognizing both the limits of the law and the goodness of marital life, the original Lutherans were sharply critical of the medieval church's sexual regulations. "Experience has shown," they wrote, "how little it is possible to improve on nature." In the 16th century, the celibacy requirement was systematically broken, making hypocrites of those required to take the vows and leaving behind a long line of victims. Women caught up in such relationships were denied the protection of law; their children were stigmatized. As the Lutherans saw it, celibacy can be a gift of the Holy Spirit given for some extraordinary purpose; where that gift is not granted, even if the vows are externally kept, the power of creaturely longing expresses itself in other ways.

Two Kingdoms

Beginning from God's justifying work in Christ Jesus, Luther drew another distinction, between two kingdoms, two realms or two different ways in which God lays claim to creation and creature. One is the kingdom that comes in the preaching of Jesus, his death and resurrection — a decisive turn in the distribution of power in which God wrests back dominance from sin, death and the devil. This kingdom extends from the present into the future. It comes now, "when God gives us his Holy Spirit so that we may believe his word and live godly lives…" as Luther puts it in the *Small Catechism*, and it will come "in heaven forever," when the forces of desolation are destroyed.

At the same time, God exerts his claim through another kingdom, composed of the various cultural assumptions, relationships, institutions, systems and structures of this life. While these forms can't bring in the new future, "the new age," as the New Testament calls it, they are a necessary part of life as we know it and accomplish all kinds of good. With other loosely associated forms of power and influence, they make up the earthly realm — the kingdom of this world. Through them, God works order, making the provisions necessary to approximate justice and peace.

Though Lutherans don't talk about it as commonly as Luther did, there is also a third, more elusive or shadowy kingdom in which the evil one and the forces of death seek to recover the control won by Christ Jesus in his death and resurrection. The devil seeks this goal by confusing the two kingdoms — by deluding us into thinking that God's rule frees Christians from the responsibilities of everyday life, for example, or by making human institutions ultimate. The third, shadowy kingdom gives itself away by its use of craft or deceit.

The two kingdoms can also be distinguished by the means God uses in them. God's rule in Christ comes through the gospel, whether in its preached or sacramental form. Through this word, the Holy Spirit creates faith, a free and merry confidence that fears, loves and trusts God above all things, as Luther puts it. All the other relationships and institutions in everyday life — the agencies of the earthly kingdom — depend upon the law and in that context, accomplish their purposes. The family, the church as an organization, various levels of government, the economy and the like are all maintained by cooperation, generally some degree of submission or obedience, just rewards or mutual respect and support.

The two kingdoms distinction sets a critical principal for believers to guard against the wily ways in which they can get confused. When ultimate claims are made by human agencies — in the state, the church or the family — they have to be brought back down to earth. At the same time, the two kingdoms distinction helps to protect the goodness and integrity of creaturely relationships. Grasped by the Spirit in true faith, believers serves freely in both kingdoms, joyfully speaking the word, delightfully loving the neighbor.

Focusing on vocation

Describing how this works, the original Lutherans focused particularly on four relationships or callings, giving them particularly close attention because they are life-creating or life-sustaining and so the decisive points of Christian service. Life is formed and shaped in the family. Work, whether it grows out of family responsibilities or gets carried out for gainful employment, is in all but the most unusual circumstances, the point where people become directly helpful in the community. The church, besides being a gathering around word and sacrament, is what has sometimes been called "an intermediate sociological structure" — an organization where people meet and care for one another, serving the larger community and the world in life-giving ways. Citizenship, while it is commonly rough and ready, less intimate than the family, a looser bond than the church, unites people in the public services required for community life — schools, governance, the quest for justice and peace. There are many other relationships in which service is rendered, but these four are the basic. In each of them plus other more particular points, God calls the faithful to the specific responsibilities of the love of the neighbor.

This service to life rendered in the callings doesn't happen simply because of people's commitments. In fact, given the continuing force of the third kingdom, people suffer some of the deepest wounds of life in their families, get taken advantage of at work, vow never to go to another annual meeting of a congregation and wonder if there is such a thing as good government. But in each of these relationships, in all of the more specific vocations believers serve, God has set things up so that there is service, voluntary or involuntary. Even such a simple act as buying a quart of milk sends out ripples of benefit: to the farm family, the dairy, the store and its staff, the people who gather around the table to drink it. All vocations are turned towards service, with or without our aid.

So the vocations are the locations of Christian service. Sometimes it is free and joyful, believers going about their duties with virtually no awareness of the good resulting — giving themselves selflessly in their families, delighting in a job well done, contributing of themselves to the congregation, rejoicing in the privileges of citizenship. Sometimes the service is begrudged and hidden, God using a calling to wring some good out of a reluctant saint who will only do as much as absolutely has to be done. But God is at work, in Luther's language, using the creature as a hand or a channel through which goodness flows or a "mask" behind which God can hide to continue, unobserved, caring for the creation.

Implications

Sorting through original Lutheran sources reinforces their place in the ecumenical consensus of the church in matters of sexual practice. Both Scripture and the church's tradition insist that God gave sexuality for marriage. Any form of mutual genital activity outside of marriage is prohibited. That said, however, there are some other clear implications in the sources.

First, when the justification of the godless is the first and last word, the center that holds Lutheran thinking together, the lines dividing the unrighteous from the righteous get blurred. "Anything that does not proceed from faith is sin," Paul says (Romans 14:23); in this life, as we know it, sin is not an occasional act but a condition in which everyone is implicated. That is as true for heterosexuals as for those who identify themselves as homosexuals. It is not a question of the really righteous versus the genuinely sinful. In a fallen world, sinners have to deal with other sinners. The absolution, the oral declaration of the forgiveness of sins, is God's word for all.

It is especially important to emphasize the forgiveness of sins in sexual matters. As many biblical stories indicate, sexuality has always been a difficult part of human relations, subject to all kinds of abuse. For countless people, women and men, sexual matters involve their deepest intimacies and wounds, ecstatic joys and profound disappointments. In virtually any conversation, there will be victims living in a hell of sorrow. If the word of forgiveness isn't given its proper place, the law will just take over, compounding itself to destroy.

Secondly, while the law can never be granted the last word, it still has a word about the shape of life. Because we are creatures who do not have life within ourselves as a possession but receive it from others, some relationships are normative: the relationship of wife and husband as well as between parents and children. By the goodness of God, life can and does continue even as these relationships are breached. But by the same token, because sexuality is so basic to these life giving relationships, it can never be regarded either a private right or a personal privilege. Heterosexual or homosexual, the sexual partner is always somebody's son or somebody's daughter, a brother or sister, who also stands under the obligation of law.

Because sexual relationships are so inherently public, the Commandments place desire under scrutiny. God uses it for good. Yet desire can also become profoundly destructive. For this reason, the experience of desire for mutual genital activity with another person or people cannot be regarded as an entitlement, as though a person has an inherent right to act it out. Neither does the persistence of such desire provide a positive basis of personal identity that entitles a person to special recognition by the community. In fact, for all of the blessing that it can be, desire also contains a threat that has to be disciplined.

Thirdly, marriage and the family is one of the defining callings, blessed by God. The words of Genesis, "be fruitful and multiply, fill the earth and subdue it" (1:28), are biblical and for that reasons, have a normative standing in the life of the church. Similarly, the God of Scripture has blessed marriage in a way that no other form of human companionship has been blessed. But neither the command to fruitfulness nor the blessing is particularly religious, mere ideas or concepts the original Lutherans picked out to impose on others. They have to do with the basic shape of life itself. From the beginning, however that beginning is conceived, women and men have united to create and care for their offspring, which has been the blessing of their union. The uniting may have been pleasant or hateful; the blessing may have been profoundly satisfying or had all the appearance of a curse; because of some other form of blessing or as a result of some evil, any number of people have not wanted to have anything to do with either the uniting or the offspring. But life cannot happen without some provision for and some protection of the relationship between the sexes.

Fourthly, as an institution of the earthly kingdom, the church has both the right and the duty to set standards appropriate to itself. Gathering a membership, collecting offerings, occupying a space along a street or road, the church is a public institution. So, like other similar organizations, it establishes policies and sets out expectations for its membership and its officers.

The *Augsburg Confession* defines two standards for the ministry. In Article V, it describes ministry as an office established by the Holy Spirit for the preaching of the word and the administration of the sacraments. In Article XIV, the authority of the office is limited by a proper call, which is the condition of a pastor's service.

The authority of ministry

American Lutherans have debated the interpretation of these articles. Some traditions have emphasized the word *office*, arguing that since God established the office, it has a prior authority of its own. Others have emphasized the word *call*, insisting that the authority of the ministry derives from the election of the congregation. In either case, whether handed down from above or granted from below, the authority of the ministry does not belong to the person who holds the office. Like anyone else who gets elected to a public office, a pastor leaves private life behind to exercise the authority necessary to carry out the assigned responsibilities for the church. Nobody has a right to ministry. As an office of the church, it belongs to the church, which has to be emphasized as strongly as possible.

Historically there have been differences in the manner of electing pastors. Some Lutherans have wanted to give greater authority to the bishop who nominates candidates for call; others have wanted to protect congregational prerogatives. Either way, there is no proper call without the congregation's consent. So candidates are considered, preparation and experience are assessed, a vote is taken and a call is issued. In its most common, printed form used among Lutherans, the call states various standards to which, as a condition of the office, the pastor agrees.

A sexual standard

One of the standards is sexual. As preachers of the word and administrators of the sacrament, pastors commonly deal with people at times of deep vulnerability — in circumstances of birth and death, in situations of illness and personal need as well as celebration and thanksgiving. This gives pastors a peculiar combination of authority and intimacy, so that people will speak with them in a way that they talk to no one else, whether family or friend. In such close relations, it is very easy for feelings to develop that cross the sexual lines.

For this reason, the office of ministry by its very nature requires sexual reliability and accountability. A pastor who uses either the authority of the office or the intimacy that it creates to become involved in mutual genital activity with another person compromises herself or himself, the other person and the office. In fact, in the experience of the church with such violations, the breach of office remains after the offending pastor leaves and will likely be detrimental for the next two or three pastors who are called to that congregation.

In the larger public life, the rough and ready of common citizenship, a person's sexual behavior may be a matter of personal choice. But when a pastor accepts a call, the pastor's sexual behavior becomes a legitimate concern of the public institution that has elected to issue the call. In fact, where the church has neglected to maintain these standards, state legislatures and the courts have increasingly stepped in to enforce their own visions of sexual reliability. The State of Minnesota, for example, requires a background check of a pastor's sexual behavior over several years prior to call. When various state courts have ruled, they have commonly held synodical and national church bodies responsible for the sexual behavior of offending clergy, resulting in settlements that run in the hundreds of thousands of dollars. A society that routinely scrutinizes the sex life of its politicians can hardly be expected to discount such concerns for the clergy.

The same standards of sexual reliability that apply to heterosexual clergy come into play with the issue of the ordination of active homosexuals. In its current statement of *Vision and Expectations* for the clergy, the ELCA has made a distinction between orientation and practice — pastors claiming a homosexual orientation may be called to congregations provided that they remain celibate. Gay and lesbian clergy have challenged this policy, appealing to some of the original Lutheran sources to argue that celibacy is no more appropriate or realistic for them than it is for heterosexual clergy. In fact, homosexual advocates have argued that traditional Christian standards of fidelity can't be applied to gays and lesbians because of differences in practice. Either way, given the church's standards and the holdings of state courts, all clergy are legally responsible for their sexual practices. If the church does change its policies on ordination, homosexual clergy will have to be willing to give a legally defensible account of their sexual practices. At the same time, the synods and the national church will have to be able to satisfy the courts that they have effectively monitored the sexual behavior of the clergy.

The Lutheran social ethic

Culling out bits and pieces of the Lutheran heritage, especially as it involves the gospel and the Commandments along with the most basic distinctions, provides orientation for discussing the issue of homosexual practice. But such a procedure also involves some risks. One is the reliability of the selection, given sinners' predilections for bias; another is changing times. The Lutheran reformers lived a long time ago; 450 to 500 years makes a difference.

Generally, the church has taken on these problems through its teachers. Theologians have worked their way through the tradition, arguing different ways in which the teachings of the reformation apply now and debating one another's findings. A good example, generally considered reliable, is a separately published volume from a larger work of a German theologian, Helmut Thielicke, entitled *The Ethics of Sex*.

As helpful as individual work might be, however, in dealing with a public issue, it is crucial to get beyond personalities and scholarly arguments to a corporate way of thinking that has been studied and refined over a period of time by people who have been called together by the church for this purpose. In the heritage of the ELCA, one of the merging churches developed such a public way of applying the Lutheran heritage to current ethical problems. In fact, its value has been examined closely and recognized for its service to the larger church in such matters. This method has been summed up in the following three statements:

First, that there is no sphere of life which is a law unto itself, autonomous of the absolute sovereignty of God, however free it must remain from ecclesiastical domination. Secondly, that all persons, apart from Christ, are capable of high degree of social justice in the building of a peaceful and humane society in which the Christian offers his or her critical co-operation and responsible participation. Thirdly, that it is in and through the personal and corporate witness of his faithful followers in their civic vocations, as well as their church worship, that Christ's lordship — however hidden in its servant form — is made manifest in our communal life in contemporary society.

Each of these statements is helpful on the issue of homosexual behavior.

Individual and Community

First, one of the major differences between the time of the Lutheran Reformation and contemporary American public life is a change in proportion between society and the individual. In the 16th century, life was inherently communal, one of the concerns of the reformers being to find a legitimate place for the individual. The founders of the American republic continued that quest in their own way, writing into the Declaration of Independence the conviction that by nature, every person has a right to life, liberty and the pursuit of happiness. The technological advances of the 20th century turned the proportions. Where the Reformers moved from the community to the individual, now the issue is moving from the individual to the public. In fact, given the rights of the individual, there is a common conviction that life is so inherently individual that the community has no legitimate voice.

Recently, this way of thinking has also been applied to sexual matters. *Roe v. Wade* — the still controversial Supreme Court decision on abortion — established legal precedent for what many people now take as a given, arguing that sexuality is a personal matter, a right to be protected from communal regulation. The church has generally followed suit. So on numerous familial and sexual issues, Lutherans have either backed off of historic ethical standards — divorce regulations, for example — or simply remained silent. Thus while parish pastors describe a social transformation in which the largest majority of couples live together prior to marriage, the church has formally said little or nothing.

These cultural arguments are now being made on the issue of homosexual practice. Sexuality is a matter of personal preference, it is said, or a result of genetic and other forms of determination that takes it beyond choice for the individual. Consequently, the church has no business continuing its opposition to gay and lesbian sexual expressions. Instead, it should bless committed homosexual relationships and ordain practicing homosexuals.

Cultures involve shared assumptions about the most basic relationships of life, sexual and otherwise. Such values are an essential part of the earthly realm; they are means through which God works for the sake of justice and peace, the ordering of public life. For that reason, Lutherans have generally viewed cultural matters positively; by the same token, Lutherans have commonly, though not always, been very critical of the church's desire to dominate the culture. As Luther is supposed to have said, "better a wise Turk than a stupid Christian," that is, better to have someone in charge that really knows what is going on than to submit to pious pretense.

This acknowledged, however, the first statement in the summary of the contemporary Lutheran social ethic points to a fundamental conflict. Though the culture may define sexuality as a personal right beyond the community's reach, Lutherans have historically insisted, "…no sphere of life is a law unto itself, autonomous of the absolute sovereignty of God…." There are a couple of basic reasons for the church's continued disagreement with the culture in sexual matters.

To begin with, the deep change in public sexual mores in the US has not and cannot eliminate the public dimension of sexuality. Birth control and the privatization of personal life have dramatically changed the way that people think about sexual relations—it is no longer true that sexual intimacy necessarily involves the possibility of child bearing. By the very conditions of human life, however, the individual cannot be sexually autonomous, but is of necessity part of the larger community: a family with its heritage, friends of the family, the community that supports it, the larger public. Withdrawal from such relationships doesn't nullify them—it just drives the connections underground where, even if not immediately noticed, they exercise their influence. The web of human interdependence that shapes life makes sexual autonomy impossible. Accordingly, the community has not only the right but also the duty to set standards.

There is a strange contradiction at this point, the kind often found in a rough and tumble of cultural values. Those who have commonly argued for the dismissal of traditional sexual standards have at the same time, strongly supported the closer regulation of the way people relate to one another in corporate life—in the work place and in schools, for example—to protect against unwelcome sexual advances. One way or another, the community plays a part.

The claim of Christ

But for the church, there is another deeper level of concern. Life in Christ is at the same time inextricably, life in community. The Holy Spirit, who calls through the gospel also and at the same time, gathers, to use the words of Luther's *Small Catechism*. As the Apostle Paul writes in Romans 14:7-8, "We do not live to ourselves, and we do not die to ourselves. If we live, we live to the Lord, and if we die, we die to the Lord; so then, whether we live or whether we die, we are the Lord's." The risen Christ lays claim to us in all of our relationships, including the sexual. Under Christ's claim, in faith we are turned towards the neighbor in a love that "hopes all things, endures all things" (1 Corinthians

13:7). The language of rights and the language of love are mutually exclusive — rights are established to preserve entitlements; love brings people together in mutual consideration.

But now this argument cuts both ways. On the one side, it stands against those who insist that cultural assumptions be imposed within the church. In fact, the culture does have integrity of its own. Standards do vary in the different cultures of the world as people attempt to come to terms with the relationships that define them. There is something provisional about these standards — they can and should change, a fact that has to be respected. But the church has its own way of thinking, shaped around the death and resurrection of Jesus of Nazareth. In that logic, sexual self-assertion, the claim to entitlement, a demand for personal or communal submission, the multiplication of partners, the subordination of the other to self-fulfillment are all suspect on any terms. In fact, the desire to place the self beyond judgment — to become one's own creator, to gain control over creation, creature and Creator for this purpose — is sin itself, no matter what the circumstance.

At the same time that it cuts against the assertion of autonomy, however, this way of thinking centers on God's call to the neighbor. If the languages of rights and love are mutually exclusive, love and dominance are also contraries. The Christ who lays claim to the bodies of the faithful is the one, now risen from the dead, who had a way of finding people who had been pushed to the margins. While none of these people in the Gospels is explicitly identified as gay or lesbian, they are again and again those — the woman at the well, for example, or the woman taken in adultery — whose sexuality had become a crucifixion. If love is deaf to the language of power, it can certainly hear and recognize the calls of those who have been marginalized or abused.

This is a particularly important consideration with families. Citizenship, the church and the family feature different kinds of relationships. So people don't expect the same of other citizens that they do of one another as church members; by the same token, as close as the Christian community becomes, it isn't as tight as a family and shouldn't be. Recognizing this, the church has to respect the advocacy of families supporting one of their own who has asserted a gay or lesbian identity. At the same time, families have to recognize that church relationships have an integrity of their own; while caring for its gay and lesbian members individually, the church as a community may have to set and maintain different policies for those who hold office within it.

Working together for Good

"You meant it for evil," Joseph said to his brothers, when they had cooked up a story to protect themselves after their father Jacob's death, "God used it for good" (Genesis 50:20). Because the forgiveness of sins blurs the line between insider and outsider, the righteous and the unrighteous, Lutherans have wanted like Joseph to emphasize the goodness God can accomplish through others, even if their intentions are questionable. So the second statement in the summary of a contemporary Lutheran social ethic holds "...that all persons, apart from Christ, are capable of high degree of social justice in the building of a peaceful and humane society in which the Christian offers his or her critical cooperation and responsible participation."

Considering a change in its policies, the church has first of all a responsibility to get an accurate analysis of the standing of gays and lesbians in public life. As usual, this has a way of turning difficult, becoming much more complicated than advocates on either side of the issue want to allow. Both proponents and opponents of change have commonly generalized from anecdotes or stereotypes, using little or no evidence to support their claims.

The reality of victims

An example of the difficulty, along with an illustration of the importance of factual date, appears in the most recent statistics gathered by the Center for Disease Control in Atlanta. The center reports three deaths of homosexuals in the last year resulting from hate crimes. During the same year, 7,000 died as the result of unprotected sex between males. No doubt, both sides will have their own interpretation of the data, but the statistics do shed some light. Opponents of a changed policy will have to acknowledge the reality of victims, even if they want to put the numbers in proportion. By the same token, while pointing out that AIDS is an equal opportunity killer, afflicting heterosexuals and homosexuals, proponents of changing the church's stand will have to acknowledge the large number of deaths does indicate a problem.

Either way, because the church has a legal responsibility for its clergy, it cannot work on suppositions, projections and possibilities—it has to recognize and address the evidence or face the public consequences. Dealing with the hard realities may not resolve the question. But it will put the church in a position to answer for itself.

At the same time, secondly, the statement of a contemporary Lutheran social ethic points out the importance of making positive assumptions about the opposition. Here again, there have been transgressors on both sides. On one, there is a long history of hateful, prejudicial treatment of gays and lesbians that has be acknowledged and confessed. On the other, the appropriation of gospel language such as "Reconciled in Christ" for gay and lesbian advocacy implicitly places those who disagree on the outside.

Whatever stance is taken, in discussions among Lutherans, there is a basis for making positive assumptions about the other. God has shaped our vocations in such a way that all people contribute to the public good, in one way or another. And in fact, both those who support a change in the church's policies and those who oppose have their contribution to make in public life, whether in the larger society or the church itself.

The Lordship of Christ Jesus

Finally, the summary of a contemporary Lutheran social ethic indicates "...that it is in and through the personal and corporate witness of his faithful followers in their civic vocations, as well as their church worship, that Christ's lordship—however hidden in its servant form—is made manifest in our communal life in contemporary society."

As a political institution, a gathering of people assembled out of public life, the church shares characteristics with every other human enterprise. It applies standards and votes policies, it accomplishes goals and also sometimes fails to meet its objectives; it is sometimes at peace and occasionally gets embroiled in conflict within itself. Putting it in comparison with the other voluntary institutions of public life, it is hard to see any noticeable difference between the church and the others.

But finally, even its various divisions, the church is united around the conviction that there is another at work within it, the triune God, justifying the godless to restore both creature and creation to the relationships intended. For this purpose, God speaks a word of judgment on the sinners assembled. The Holy Spirit becomes the user of the law, calling into question the seemingly endless self-absorption of sinners who, turned in on themselves, seek to become a law unto themselves. But the word of judgment is preliminary to the last word, a word that is also ultimately the Holy Spirit's responsibility. It is the gospel, the word of pardon and release in Christ Jesus, the word of forgiveness and resurrection, finally, a word of freedom.

It is a different kind of freedom. The freedom rightfully celebrated in American public life is political—it is freedom of choice, the freedom of self-determination. The freedom of the gospel is freedom from choice, freedom to enter irretrievably into the defining relationships of every-day life in service to the neighbor. These relationships all involve a cross. To be part of a family, to go to work day after day, to be shaped by a congregation, to take up the duties of citizenship under the conditions of life as we know it, necessarily involves self-loss. But in these daily deaths, in this dying with Christ, there is also the hope of a resurrection like his. So in the *hiddeness* of the ordinary, in the encumbrances and contrariness of everyday responsibility, the good Lord takes hold of our bodies — hands, feet and other members — to create the new future. Occasionally, in the deepest relationships of life, there are glimpses of what will be — in the tenderness that breaks through the hostilities that have divided people, for example, or in a quiet re-assurance granted amidst suffering. Such glimpses, however, move the faithful from the eye to the ear, to the word — whether in its preached or sacramental form — which bespeaks the new age dawning.

For all of its foibles, for all of its limitations, for all of its implications in the injustices of the world, the church is in the end a creature of God's word. It exists and can only continue in this purpose. As Lutherans have heard it, this word realizes itself in a freedom that holds under the cross for the sake of the resurrection. That is a word for all, even if considerations of policy require placing limits on institutional endorsements and office holders.

Final issues

Given these considerations of the Lutheran heritage, in its original form and as interpreted and applied more recently by Lutherans, there are three issues that require examination as the church debates its policy of homosexual practice.

The first is ecumenical. Even after Luther's excommunication, the original Lutherans saw themselves as belonging within the Catholic tradition of the church. That tradition, which includes the vast majority of the world's Christians, continues to hold standards on homosexual practice that it understands to be required by Scripture and the faith itself. Though various individual interpreters have offered personal interpretations of the biblical passages involved, the church's ecumenical authorities have shown little indication of a willingness to change the historic standards or to regard them as a matter in which they are willing to accept difference. Debating its current policies, the ELCA will have to consider that endorsing practicing homosexuals by blessings or ordination would isolate it from the ecumenical consensus and alienate it from the very church bodies with which it has sought closer accords.

Secondly, while cultural standards on sexual matters have changed dramatically in recent decades, increasingly strict legal provisions have been put in place to closely regulate the sexual behavior of clergy. Under this rule of law, gays and lesbians seeking to practice their homosexuality while serving as clergy will have to be willing to provide a public accounting of their sexual relationships. The church, both synodically and nationally, will have to decide whether it is willing to assume with homosexuals the legal and financial responsibility that the law has already imposed on it for monitoring the sexual practices of heterosexual clergy.

Thirdly, in the issues of blessing gay and lesbian unions and ordaining practicing homosexuals, there is a fundamental conflict between cultural and traditional Christian views of sexuality. Contemporary culture has privatized sexual relationships, regarding them as a matter of personal desire and therefore of right and entitlement. Lutherans, in the context of the larger Catholic tradition, have regarded sexuality as inextricably tied to the vocation of the family, so as a matter of honoring and cherishing the other and the community.

Neither Evangelical nor Lutheran

In, with and under these three issues, intertwined among them, another matter shows through — the defining issue for Lutherans. Using another person for sexual self-gratification, with or without consent, reduces the other to an object or an occasion—a serious enough problem by itself, no matter how or where it happens. But in the original Lutheran ways of thinking, the fundamental point is always justification by faith. Seeking life in "creatures, saints and devils"—trying to find the significance or value of one's self on personal terms, attempting to establish an identity beyond God's judgment, is idolatry. In an older language, it is "justification by works," whether the doings are religious or apparently irreligious, pious or profligate.

The church exists for one purpose, to declare Holy Absolution, to speak Christ's forgiving word, the justification of the godless in its preached and sacramental forms. There has always been a special dimension to this promise for those who have been caught up in their own sexuality. So the ELCA has committed itself to a special welcome for gays and lesbians. But just for that reason, just because of the justification wrought in Christ Jesus, the church has to challenge all of the other justification schemes that are offered. Having examined the Lutheran heritage, in its early writings and its authoritative interpretation, it is impossible to avoid the conclusion drawn by Wolfhart Pannenberg from the biblical evidence. A leading ecumenical theologian, he holds that a church that rejects the traditional teaching on homosexual practice cannot be either evangelical or Lutheran, no matter what it calls itself.

James A. Nestingen is professor of church history at Luther Seminary, St. Paul, Minnesota. A nationally recognized Luther scholar as well as a popular speaker and lecturer, he is the author of numerous books, including The Faith We Hold; Martin Luther: His Life and His Writings; Roots of Our Faith; *and* Manger in the Mountains.

For Further Reading

Bornkamm, Heinrich. *Luther on the Old Testament.* Eric and Ruth Gritsch, translators; Victor I. Gruhn, editor. Philadelphia: Fortress Press, 1969.

Lazareth, William H. *Christians in Society: Luther, the Bible and Social Ethics.* Minneapolis: Fortress, 2001.

Luther, Martin. "The Small Catechism" and "The Large Catechism," in Robert Kolb and Timothy R. Wengert, editors, *The Book of Concord.* Minneapolis: Fortress Press, 2000.

Thielicke, Helmut. *The Ethics of Sex.* New York: Harper and Row, 1964.

Wingren, Gustaf. *Luther on Vocation.* Carl C. Rasmussen, translator. Philadelphia: Muhlenberg Press, 1957.

 Chapter Three

Some Thoughts from a Pastor Who Serves as a Bishop

By Thomas A. Skrenes

The biblical faith

It was my first Sunday in my first call. I was a 25-year-old seminary graduate, not yet ordained. The worship service had gone very well and frankly, I was pleased with the sermon and the way I had conducted the liturgy. After worship I was shaking hands at the back of the church and a little girl, blonde and five years old walked up to me. She grabbed my alb and pulled on my cincture. Putting her hands on her hips, she said to me: "Say, whatever happened to the other Jesus."

It was at that point that I knew what ministry and even Christianity was all about. We who are baptized, we who are ordained are called to represent Jesus Christ to the church and to the world. We are called, somehow, to be in the world but not of it. We are called to be in the likeness of Jesus, to act like Jesus.

The way we learn to be like Jesus Christ is through the Scriptures. We hold the Bible to be the Word of God. In the ordination service of our church we say this:

> The Church in which you are to be ordained confesses that the Holy Scriptures are the Word of God and are the norm of its faith and life. We accept, teach, and confess the Apostles', the Nicene, and the Athanasian Creeds. We also acknowledge the Lutheran Confessions as true witnesses and faithful expositions of the Holy Scriptures. Will you therefore preach and teach in accordance with the Holy Scriptures and these creeds and confessions?[1]

The crisis of Biblical faith is one of ignorance and apathy. I am always visiting congregation councils in my work. I sit with call committees, I work with stewardship committees; I try to assist congregations when there is a dispute within the parish — usually between a pastor and a congregation council. Again and again I am amazed how little the scriptures and its teachings are valued by many of our people. Many of our congregations have little or no adult Bible study in place whatsoever. It is not unusual for congregation council meetings to begin with the briefest of prayer or devotions and then get down to the "real business" of the church. When congregational leaders do not study the Bible or participate in Christian study, when personal opinions trump the Scriptures, we are sick as a church. We must pray that this spiritual malaise, this illness, is not unto death.

The danger in interpreting the Scriptures in any way we choose is that the gospel we preach and the way we live begins to look like something else than Jesus. I am convinced that we cannot twist the Scriptures to say anything we want them to say. To pretend that the Word of God approves of certain types of homosexual relationships is to be fundamentally wrong. We cannot change the Biblical concepts of marriage and family to whatever we want them to be. I have been using Martin Luther's *Small Catechism* in my teaching and preaching. This treasure says it best when brother Luther explains the Sixth Commandment, "You shall not commit adultery."

> What is this? Answer: We are to fear and love God, so that we lead pure and decent lives in word and deed, and each of us loves and honors his or her spouse.[2]

My struggle

One question I have struggled with is this. What if I am wrong? What if the recognition of homosexuality is the human rights issue of our time? What if I am wrong and this issue is really one of justice, and the Holy Spirit is leading us one step more on the road to human freedom and enlightenment? What if being a gay person is no different than being left-handed? I take very seriously that possibility. Is my hubris the sin here and not homosexual activity?

However, when I think on all of this, I am hit right between the eyes with the words of Jesus from Matthew's Gospel:

> If anyone should cause one if these little ones to lose his faith in me, it would be better for that person to have a large mill-

stone tied around his neck and be drowned in the deep sea. (Matthew 18:6)

As a pastor and bishop of this church I cannot stand by while the word of God is manipulated, explained away or worse yet ignored. I must follow the dictates of my conscience as formed by the Scriptures and traditions of the church. Those who advocate a change in our current practices regarding the ordination of non-celibate homosexuals and the blessing of same sex unions have not convinced me. If I can be convinced by the Word of God that I am wrong — so be it. I will then change my opinion on this matter. But that has not happened.

The culture

As a Christian, I am convinced that the crisis in sexual ethics is much broader than homosexual relationships. By all accounts, same sex relationships involve less than one in ten persons. The crisis in sexual ethics is the failure to see sexuality as God intends for God's people. The crisis is the compromise with the secular practices of our time. The crisis is the normalization of those practices amongst our people.

The church is a part of the culture, and we in this church seem to be as confused as the rest of the world about how to live as sexual human beings. Congregational leaders and pastors are not teaching Biblical sexual ethics. Pastors do not preach about marriage. Marriage is understood in this culture, and too often in the Church, as a personal decision with few consequences for the community. The Church has failed to teach Christian sexual ethics. And now that failure to articulate a solid understanding of sexuality, marriage and family is erupting in our time as a discussion on the ethical normality of homosexual practice. Indeed the chickens are coming home to roost! The current struggle that the whole church is engaged in is the result of our failure to know what Scripture says about marriage and sexuality and then the failure to make that teaching, in the words of our own church constitutions, "the authoritative source and norm of its proclamation, faith, and life."

Ask any parish pastor in my synod or in yours about the normal state of premarital life. It is "living together." It seems almost quaint to call that non-marital cohabitation, "living in sin." Not only for those who are under 30 years of age but in all age brackets, the social stigma attached to pre-marital sexual relationships has nearly vanished. One pastor told me recently that he has in three years of ministry yet to join in marriage a couple who were not living together. The exceptional has become, in the past decades, the normal. And now living together before marriage is more than normal. It has become the expected.

This year children born to parents who are not married total one-third of all births in the United States. In our rural Upper Peninsula of Michigan and the north woods of Wisconsin, we exceed the national rate. In all things sexual, what was once exceptional has become normal.

Psychologist and therapist William Pinsof is president of The Family Institute at Northwestern University and director of its Center for Applied Psychological and Family Studies. His new analysis of family appeared in the respected *Family Process Journal*. It reflects the normalization of the formerly exceptional. Pinsof writes:

> Divorce should be regarded as one of the normal social events in the life course of modern families. Living together should be seen as a legitimate end-state in itself.[3]

So how does the church of Jesus Christ speak to this issue? How do we as a part of the Christian community address this huge change in the values and behaviors of our families? The church seems not to have a message here. It is pretty quiet out there. Our church has yet to find a voice.

Writing of the curious silence in regards to sexual ethics, Pastor Phillip Max Johnson has written in *Lutheran Forum* this powerful critique of all of us in the church:

> We are so compromised by our pastoral silence regarding sexual behavior, so embarrassed by our personal failures, so jaded by the general ethical chaos, that clarity or courage on the matter of homosexuality seems out of reach ... The "need" for sexual expression, the quasi-religious status granted to romantic love, the "right" to happiness, the shrinking of marriage down to the single dimension of mutual happiness, the general separation of sexual love from fecundity, the naturalization of lust: these cultural orthodoxies and influences hem us in. The call to chastity can be heard only as the imposing of a cruel and unusual punishment. [4]

Church unity

Those who advocate a change in the current practice of our church to permit ordination of non-celibate gay and lesbian persons are well entrenched and well funded. They probably do not represent a majority of the laity of this church but may represent a majority of key decision makers.

Gary Wills is an author and journalist. In his superb book *Certain Trumpets* he writes about leadership and the power of a determined minority within democratic institutions:

> Not many people will vote with their whole lives–give their days and nights, their money and influence, to a single cause. But those who do have a disproportionate impact on society, as one would expect from their investment of energy and conviction, as compared with the lukewarm or diffident commitment of others. This is why intense minorities often prevail over lackadaisical majorities in a democracy.[5]

This issue of homosexual acceptance amongst our clergy, albeit championed by a minority in the whole church, may become accepted by our church, that is our democratic church, expressed in national assemblies.

An activist minority can make all the difference. St. Paul-Reformation Lutheran Church of St. Paul, Minnesota states in a June 2002 letter to the bishops of this church that it has a budget of $116,445 to distribute a videotape entitled *This Obedience* which it plans to send to each voting member of the ELCA assembly. In their letter to me requesting funds for this project, this movement has decided to make this issue a justice and even faith-centered question. It is being thus elevated to a doctrinal question. The letter says, "The best ways to change minds in the fight for spiritual equality is though the personal stories and journeys of our Gay Lesbian Bisexual and Transgendered brothers and sisters."[6]

How much money, how much energy will be expended to obtain the desired political outcome at the decision making conventions or assemblies. Does anyone doubt that in many synods, there will be slates of candidates advanced with this one agenda item in mind? Does anyone doubt that there will be those going to these meetings who will be there only to change the current practice? Does anyone doubt that there will be those going who will be there only to vote to retain our current practice?

Marginalizing option

It is clear to me that if the church accepts the ordination of non-celibate homosexuals what will follow is the marginalization and finally the proscription of any teaching of sexual ethics that does not include homosexual activity as a viable option. And those of us who do not find homosexual activity as God-pleasing will at first, unofficially but eventually officially, be placed in the same category as Lutheran racists of fifty years ago or those who opposed women's ordination in a generation past. Candidacy committees will soon eliminate candidates for ordination who believe that the Scriptures do not approve of homosexuality. Our seminary faculties will soon face a theological "litmus test" of a new homosexual orthodoxy. All of this will happen very quickly. And those who believe that homosexual activity is wrong will be, in short order, considered fundamentalists.

Pastor Leonard Klein has done us all a service by articulating the questions that must be asked if this church is to sanction committed homosexual relationships. If we as a church body bless these unions or allow pastors to live in such so called committed relationships, questions need to be asked. Klein writes:

> How will the ELCA know what a committed relationship is, when it has begun, or when it has ended? ...Will parishes be expected to consider partnered gay candidates on the same basis with other candidates for call? Will they be denied candidates if they refuse? ... Or will the ELCA assume that Partnered Gay clergy are only to be sent to a certain subset of parishes and institutions that have said they are willing to have them? What impact would that have on the unity of the denomination? Will pastors who refuse to accept Partnered Gay clergy as fit colleagues be reprimanded, disciplined, or discriminated against in the call process? Will bishops and synods that refuse to ordain or accept Partnered Gay candidates remain in full and harmonious communion with those who do and with the ELCA as a whole? ... Will parishes be expected to allow Partnered Gay clergy and their partners to occupy the parsonage? Will they be expected to provide housing allowances that are suitable for a single person or for a couple? Will parishes be expected to accept public displays of affection between Partnered Gay clergy and their partners? To what degree? ... Will Partnered Gay clergy who break with their partners be regarded as the same as divorcing clergy? At what point will a change in partners constitute a disciplinary problem? Will it be acceptable to divorce a spouse and thereafter enter into a same-sex relationship? What about the opposite case? ... Will the church health and Pension plans extend benefits to the partners of Partnered Gay clergy? Will congregations be required to provide such benefits? What will Partnered Gay clergy be expected to preach and teach about marriage?[7]

Questions for a bishop
The last time I counted, the constitution and bylaws of my synod told me that I have 37 different responsibilities in this office as bishop. The

first one listed is to be the "synod's pastor." The second one charged to my responsibility is to "Preach, teach and administer the sacraments in accord with the Confession of Faith of this church." Reflecting on those responsibilities, listen to a few questions that come to my mind. The bishop must relate, work with and be supportive of all of her or his pastors when they are serving God faithfully. How do I support a pastor who is taking a position on this issue that I believe to be wrong? How do I walk with, serve and assist a congregation that blesses same-sex unions when I find no evidence in Scripture or in tradition for such a practice?

How do I respond to the life-long Lutheran who tells me that she will not be able to worship in a church that allows homosexual unions before God's altar? How do I counsel a celibate homosexual pastor who asks me to explain how the Word of God can be changed by an ELCA convention when he or she has spent a life time struggling with this issue and has resolved it in a very different way than has the church? Can a majority vote at an Assembly change the hearts and minds of faithful laity and clergy? As a bishop, can I honestly counsel a pastor who is having problems with a same sex partner especially since I am of the belief that God does not approve of these relationships even if a future church convention does?

As bishop and as a parent, how do I deal with my own children's pastor if she or he teaches Christian sexuality in the catechism class that is foreign to my understanding? If my children's pastor teaches a theology of sexuality that is alien to my understanding—what do I do? Shop around for a new church? If as bishop, I am too strident in my position in this issue will I be marginalized by my colleagues in the Conference of Bishop? Or will I just be "put up with" until I retire, accept a pastoral call, or until the folks in my synod see fit to replace me with someone more "progressive?" Already I have witnessed conversation on this issue quickly turn to label tossing. All who suggest that the church maintain its current status must in short order defend themselves from being called "homophobic."

Learning to talk

Will this debate divide our communion more than it is already divided? I pray not. Instead of fracture, what seems to me most likely is that whatever the issue outcome, a significant portion of this church will be alienated. Unity and financial mission support beyond the congregation, already in short supply, will further decline.

Our church needs all of us, pastors and laity, to reflect on these issues. My sense in our congregations is that there is only small interest in studying this issue. This time of journeying together will not work if our congregations are silent and then only reactive to decisions that are made by elites within the church.

Our pastors and lay leaders must learn how to talk about homosexuality. And it must be a genuine conversation with all people. If there continues to be a reservoir of avoidance amongst us on this issue, we will only face trouble in the years ahead. Can we promise ourselves that this natural resistance to deal with this issue will be overcome by us as we continue this conversation? This effort should not be a political campaign but an opportunity to listen to the Word of God and to God's people.

Facing facts

Those of us who oppose the ordination of non-celibate homosexuals also must be asked some questions. Indeed we must be willing to face facts. Do we have the courage in this church, at this time, to stand with the person who believes that she or he is homosexual in orientation? Instead of encouraging them to form a homosexual union, can we help them to remain celibate? A bishop in this church has told me that out of this debate on the ordination of non-celibate homosexual persons must come structures and methods of supporting those gay sisters and brothers who wish to remain celibate. There are pastors of this church who consider themselves gay and who believe sexual activity outside of heterosexual marriage is wrong and sinful. They are quietly calling on this church to help them remain celibate. What are we going to do? Should we tell them that their own conclusions to a lifetime of discernment and study were unnecessary or even un-Christian? Are we to say to these long struggling folks, "Sorry—the church has changed its mind. You are now free to form a gay relationship?"

Many forces are threatening to tear us apart as a church, including rampant congregationalism, materialism, and individual interpretations of the Word of God. Wilfred M. McClay, professor of Humanities at the University of Tennessee, has written on U.S. history that:

> The story of American Protestantism in particular is a vexing story of one church quarrel after another, nearly always eventuating in bitter division, mitosis without end. Which suggests why the larger story line of American religious history is the collapse of Protestant dominance, which has gradually yielded ground first to Roman Catholicism . . ., then to a vague Judeo-Christian tradition, and then to a more and more wide-

open religious pluralism, which has moved far beyond Judeo-Christian limits.[8]

One of the most beautiful prayers attributed to Luther is his Sacristy Prayer. I pray it for all of us who seek God's will for this church in this time of decision.

> Lord God, thou hast made me a pastor and teacher in the Church. Thou seest how unfit I am to administer this great and responsible office, and had I been without thy aid and counsel I would have surely ruined it long ago. Therefore do I invoke thee. How gladly do I desire to yield and consecrate my heart and mouth to this ministry, I desire to teach the congregation. I too desire ever to learn and keep thy word my constant companion and meditate thereupon earnestly. Use me as thy instrument in thy service. Only do not thou forsake me, for if I am left to myself, I would certainly bring it all to destruction. Amen.

Thomas A. Skrenes is bishop of the ELCA Northern Great Lakes Synod, elected in 1999. He is a graduate of the University of Wisconsin in Madison, Wisconsin, and Trinity Lutheran Seminary, Columbus, Ohio. Ordained in 1980, he served as pastor of Trinity Lutheran Church, Ishpeming, Michigan, and later as assistant to the bishop prior to becoming the synod bishop.

---

[1] *Occasional Services* 1982: Augsburg, page 194

[2] *Small Catechism* (Wingert translation), page 16

[3] *US Today*, July 29, 2002, page 4d

[4] Phillip Max Johnson, "Homo-Genital Love and Same-Sex Unions," *Lutheran Forum*, Summer 2002, page 16

[5] *Certain Trumpets* by Garry Wills (Simon and Schuster, 1994), page 40

[6] Letter dated June 2002 from St. Paul-Reformation Lutheran Church of St. Paul, Minnesota

[7] Leonard Klein, "Equivalent Marriage: Questions to Ask," *Forum Letter*, July 2002

[8] *A Student's Guide to U.S. History* by Wilfred M. McClay (ISI Books, Wilmington, Delaware; 2000), page 76

 # Chapter Four

Clergy and Divorce

By Russell E. Saltzman

I will begin with a series of anecdotes. Then, briefly, I will examine the biblical texts. Then, I will tell you what I think of divorce and remarriage as a theological problem, given our Lutheran theology of marriage, and offer what I hope is a faithful solution. Finally, I will make some suggestion of what to do with divorced and divorcing pastors.

Anecdotal Precedents

I will begin, as I said, with the anecdotal elements. I personally know each of the principals involved in these stories. For obvious reasons, I cannot reveal names.

The conversation was over dinner in 1987. The friend I was with was then a prominent leader in one of the merging Lutheran church bodies and instrumental in the merger conversations that led to the Evangelical Lutheran Church in America. He asked the pianist to play a certain song, and he warned me to stop talking when the piano began to play that song. The song began. Tears came to his eyes. The song ended. He explained. While on his pastoral internship, he had met and had fallen in love with a divorced woman. Her divorced status precluded any possibility of marriage if he wanted to become a pastor. "It just would not have worked," he said. "Not back then." "Back then" was in the late 1940s. If you could not be a pastor in the Lutheran church of the 1940s, 1950s, and on into the early 1960s, married to a woman previously divorced.

The woman he did marry knew nothing of the previous relationship. For reasons that escape me, I perhaps was the first person he had ever told. His had been a good life, he assured me, with a deeply satis-fying marriage, fine children, and through his position and leadership he had done great things in and for the Lutheran church. Yet for all that, his mind would wistfully return to the occasion of his first real romance, and he would always wonder.

I had an elderly parishioner, a World War II veteran, who had once in his early years thought to become a pastor. His wife, however, had deserted the marriage while he was stationed in the Pacific in 1944, admitting adultery on her part. He returned from the war, entered col-lege on the G.I. Bill, met a girl and remarried. Because he was divorced and remarried, no seminary then would entertain his application.

Come forward to 1978 and to a graduate of an American Lutheran Church seminary. While as a married student in the mid-1960s, his mar-riage was unraveling. His spouse left him briefly during that time. The best advice he received from a seminary official was, get a bottle of wine and a motel room. Work it out or drop out, were his options.

He and his spouse reconciled. He graduated, received a call, but while in his first parish, the marriage collapsed irreparably. He was compelled immediately to resign his call, as was customary. In the time he was off the clergy roster, he met and married another woman. (That marriage has happily endured.)

He was allowed to reenter parish ministry some years later, first as a part-time assistant pastor, later as a full-time pastor. But this hap-pened only after a fairly thorough and somewhat rigorous examination by the district president (in the days before we called them bishops), and after formal readmission to the clergy roster.

Still, another story — the year was 1986 and a middle-age second career seminarian, in her senior year, supply-preached at a parish. She took the occasion of her sermon to speak of her call to the ministry. Her summons to theological education and parish ministry involved, as it often does for second-career folk, a vast unraveling of home, career, and income. In this seminarian's instance, as she revealed through her sermon, her transition also entailed insurmountable strain on her mar-riage. Her husband had no desire to up-root their family and move. This was solved, she related, when their last child graduated high school, whereupon she divorced her husband and entered seminary. Her call to pastoral ministry, she believed, justified even the sacrifice of her marriage.

My final story is from 1990. A pastor is being interviewed for call. He receives the nod and accepts. However, he arrives at the congregation without his spouse, and announces, by the way, his wife will not be joining him; they are in the process of seeking a divorce. In fact, the process had been underway at the time of his interview, but he withheld that information from the call committee. This lack of candor at the outset led to a short and in some ways disastrous pastorate that continues to haunt the congregation's ministry.

A steady progression

We can see, I think, a fairly steady progression in the nature of the stories I have related. Where it was once an axiomatic expectation that no divorced pastor could remain on the clergy roster—even that no man could marry a divorced woman and become a pastor; even that no divorced person could enter seminary—we now have many divorced pastors serving on the clergy roster, some serving among the conference of bishops, and even some pastors now marking anniversaries in their third marriages.

Were I to here ask for a show of hands from divorced pastors attending this conference,[1] my hand would rise first.

I do not for one instant enjoy the *fact* of being divorced. It is biographical notation that glares at me off the page. More, there is not a day when I am not consciously aware of being divorced. It is a condition of *being* that I carry with me everywhere, at all times. In a word, and with frank candor, I find it shameful.

I have remarried. I have two children from this marriage to go along with the five children from my previous marriage. It is difficult, painful, explaining to my youngest child why my youngest son must leave our house every other weekend to go visit his mother, my previous spouse. I explain it in straight, simple language whenever she asks, but I am grateful she is yet too young to sense my embarrassment, my shame.

All that said, I must also say that having remarried, I never knew marriage could be just so much downright fun.

Wondering what has happened

We look around at our own lives as pastors, experiencing the things we experience in divorce, hearing the things we hear of colleagues, and may one rightly wonder what is happening to the Lutheran pastorate.

The short answer is what is happening to us the same thing that is happening to all marriage in Western culture. There is no reason to believe that clergy marriages are immune from the same influences that impress themselves upon our parishioners. The same stresses, fractures, desires and lusts that swirl in our culture swirl also among pastors.

Textual examination

I shall take up the biblical texts, with this warning, I find no comfort for my condition, only searing accusation.

The relevant texts begin with St. Matthew, where we find two pertinent passages.

St. Matthew 5:31-32 — "It has been said, 'Anyone who divorces his wife must give her a certificate of divorce.' But I tell you that anyone who divorces his wife, except for marital unfaithfulness, causes her to become an adulteress, and anyone who marries the divorced woman commits adultery."

St. Matthew 19:3-9 (Parallel in St. Mark 10:1-9) — Some Pharisees came to him to test him. They asked, "Is it lawful to a man to divorce his wife for any and every reason?" "Haven't you heard," he replied, "that at the beginning the Creator 'made them male and female," and said, 'For this reason a man will leave his father and mother and be united to his wife, and the two will become one flesh'? So they are no longer two, but one. Therefore what God has joined together, let man not separate."

"Why then," they asked, "did Moses command that a man giver his wife a certificate of divorce and send her away?"

Jesus replied, "Moses permitted you to divorce your wives because your hearts were hard. But it was not this way from the beginning. I tell you that anyone who divorces his wife, except for marital unfaithfulness, and marries another woman commits adultery."

St. Mark 10:1-9 (Parallel in St. Matthew 19:3-9) — Some Pharisees came and tested him by asking, "Is it lawful for a man to divorce his wife?" "What did Moses command you?" he replied. They said, "Moses permitted a man to write a certificate of divorce and send her away." "It was because your hearts were hard that Moses wrote you this law," Jesus replied. "But at the beginning of creation God 'made them male and female.' For this reason a man will leave his father and mother and be united to his wife, and the two will become one flesh. So they are no longer two, but one. Therefore what God has joined together, let man not separate."

When they were in the house again, the disciples asked Jesus about this. He answered, "Anyone who divorces his wife and marries another woman commits adultery against her. And if she divorces her husband and marries another man, she commits adultery."

St. Luke 16:18 — Anyone who divorces his wife and marries another woman commits adultery, and the man who marries a divorced woman commits adultery.

There is also First Corinthians 7:10-11 — To the married I give this command (not I, but the Lord): A wife must not separate from her husband. But if she does, she must remain unmarried or else be reconciled to her husband. And a husband must not divorce his wife.

For the purposes of this essay, St. Luke does not concern us here. The verse is consistent with Matthew and Mark, but it has no recognizably coherent context; the verse just sort of drops in from nowhere. It comes immediately after the parable of the shrewd manager, and before the story of Lazarus and the rich man. You don't know why it is there; it does make you wish St. Luke had used a better editor.

In St. Matthew there are two complimentary teachings on divorce, but arising out of two entirely different contexts. The first comes in St. Matthew's version of the Sermon on the Mount, found in chapter 5. At verse 21, Jesus begins a series of antithetical contrasts. Each is introduced by "You have heard it said" and followed with "But I say to you." Hatred is placed on a level with murder for murder arises from hatred; lust becomes adultery for adultery arises from lust; an "eye for an eye" is contrasted with "turn the other cheek"; and "love your neighbor but hate your enemy" is contrasted with "love your enemies." It is in this setting that Jesus raises the bar on marriage and closes the door to divorce and remarriage.

This comes, then, in a series of examples of how the New Spirit or the New Covenant of Christ fulfills the law and the prophets, and so produces a righteousness exceeding that of Scribes and Pharisees. What the Law demands by right, the disciple of Jesus gives freely from the heart. Divorce and adultery appear in the context of community life, of brothers and sisters seeking peace and mutual reconciliation, not through mechanical obedience, but by adherence to the spirit behind the law.

He repeats what were common interpretations of the Law of Moses, and then — by presenting a true righteousness of the heart, a "new spirit within us" — he penetrates below the surface of a legalistic understanding and announces the aim of the law rather than its letter.

Matthew 19 and Mark 10, specifically, occur in the context of a verbal contest with the Pharisees. (One presumes these were the Pharisees who missed the Sermon on the Mount.) In these two parallels Jesus argues from what is permissible under the law — what Moses permitted — is not what God intended. In Mark, Luke and First Corinthians, there is no allowance for divorce, period, and especially Jesus forbade marriage after divorce, calling it adultery. [2]

In Matthew, however, Jesus allowed divorce for adultery. In this instance he sided with the stricter rabbinical interpretation of Deuteronomy 24:1. That passage allows divorce for "some indecency." According to one school, "indecency" was just about anything in general (Hillel). Another (Shammai) said "indecency" could mean only adultery.

Along with divorce for adultery, the dissimilarity between Matthew and Mark is that Mark apparently knows of a divorce that women, too, may obtain. In some Jewish colonies outside of Palestine, influenced by Greek or Roman customs, that certainly was possible.

Bottom line, the only possible reason for divorce — from either the woman's or the man's perspective — is the unfaithfulness of the other. Until the advent of "no-fault" divorce, this was fairly enshrined in American law. There were other grounds for divorce besides adultery, but they required reasons. There are no necessary reasons today. Because we Lutherans tend to look at marriage as the business of the state, we have failed to regard it as also properly the business of the church.

A theology of marriage

Marriage, as we Lutherans have been wont to express it, is the life long union of one man to one woman. We have traditionally viewed it as an order of creation, "a structure of human life built into the creation by the Creator . . . [which] builds upon our creation as male and female." Marriage then is a naturally occurring condition among us humans simply by virtue of us being human, made in the way we are made. Marriage does not depend upon an acknowledgment of Jesus as Lord, but upon the exercise of humanity's God-given capacities for community and family clustering. All marriage is blest by God and finds favor in his sight through the gift of family. Marriage fulfills one of the purposes of creation, and the man and woman whose lives have been united as one in marriage become co-creators with God, renewing and replenishing the earth. Marriage is a means by which God's grace comes to the whole human family, irrespective of religion, race, region or culture.

Yet marriage also is to be understood as a divinely rendered institution within the vocational exercise of the baptized. Marriage is not peculiar to the church, but marriage as a Christian vocation is.[4]

Marriage becomes distinctly Christian by the name of Christ whereby it is undertaken. It is distinctively Christian through the couple's faith in the creative, sustaining love of the Father, the redemptive presence of Christ within their life together (through whose name and by whose name they forgive one another), and by the sanctifying power of the Holy Spirit (in stark contrast to all the other "spirits" that so frequently dominate marriage in our culture).

Christians in marriage seek to do in their home what the church catholic seeks to do at large throughout the world — to proclaim that love which God has shown to the world, and to make that love visible in the lives they touch and nurture. In this way, marriage becomes a celebration of Christian faith brought to fruition among believers, and the lives united as one become sacramental channels of grace.[5]

The sin of divorce

This is what God intended when he made them male and female from the beginning. But "because of sin, our age-old rebellion, the gladness of marriage can be overcast and the gift of family can become a burden."[6]

"The gladness of marriage can be overcast"? You have no idea.

The union of one man and one woman is what God wanted from the beginning. But in the hardness of our hearts, what God wants — in a world fallen into sin — is not always what God gets. Sin, death and the devil, in Martin Luther's marvelous phrase, conspire against the will of God, doing violence against what God has joined together.

Divorce violates the will of God. There is no other way in which it may be regarded. It is a moral and social calamity. I have gone over and over those texts I cited earlier. There is, it seems to me, absolutely no escape. Divorce is not merely a manifestation of sin, a consequence of sin, it is sin, period. It may be legal, as even Jesus admitted in regard to the Law of Moses, due to the hardness of our hearts, but it is never morally neutral. No matter the justification for a divorce, however "good" or necessary it may be, divorce remains sin.

An example of holy living

So we now confront these words adopted by the church council of the Evangelical Lutheran Church in America: "The ordained minister is to be an example of holy living, so that the ordained minister's life does not become an impediment to the hearing of the gospel or a scandal to the community of faith." [7]

It was exactly so, thirty years ago or less, that a divorced pastor could not be an example of holy living. This is a judgment no longer made. We have come to an informal and altogether practical accommodation. Divorced pastors are no longer an "impediment to the hearing of the gospel" and no longer "a scandal to the community of faith."

The true scandal in all of this, of course, is that divorce and remarriage are no longer a source of scandal. To put it better, divorce and remarriage are no longer a real, authentic and genuine occasion for the examination of a man or woman in ministry. Are we the better for this? The way we have handled divorce and remarriage among pastors, bluntly, is no model for any one, clergy or lay. There is even an element of collusion in sin between divorced clergy and divorced laity: don't ask about my scandal, and I won't ask about yours.

We must ask what we have not asked. In what way may a divorced pastor, remarried, be an example of holy living?

My answer is, in the same way as all repentant sinners redeemed in Christ.

Repenting of my sin

Let me go over this again. Divorce is sin, yes. It creates a continuing condition of sin, and it is public sin. In divorce, perhaps more clearly than in any other public area of life, to borrow a phrase from Martin E. Marty, "original sin daily turns into actual sin." [8]

Thus, "When our Lord and Master Jesus Christ said, 'Repent,' he willed the entire life of believers to be one of repentance." It is this "entire life of repentance"[9] which must mark all our lives, but which, I contend, must mark especially the lives of those who are ordained, but divorced.

I am keenly aware of my failures as a first husband, the things I did not do and the things I should have done that might have preserved my marriage. But thanks to my Old Adam, generally I am far more keenly aware of the things *she* should have done, and did not do, to preserve our marriage. One of my greatest shocks in the entire process of divorce and its aftermath was when a friend, a colleague, wondered aloud if I really was the best thing to have ever happened in *her* life.

This "entire life of repentance" is not a stubborn return to the scene of the crime, nor is it a vivid recitation of "by my fault, by my own fault, by my own most grievous fault," rendered *ad nauseam*. Still less is it a vivid recitation of "by her fault, by her own fault, by her own most grievous fault."

But it must be, I think, in the very first place, a true, authentic, genuine acknowledgment of sin, and not in general, but in particular, my sin. And in the second place, an equally true, authentic, genuine acknowledgment that for all our sins, and for my sin in particular, there is Christ as remedy, Christ as my daily hope for renewal of spirit and redemption from the past.

If the Lord does not "despise a broken and contrite heart," neither must the Lord's church.[10] The remedy for our circumstance and condition, in short, is confession and absolution.

In this way, bracketed always by repentance, the lives of all pastors may become "an example of holy living," without impediment to the hearing of the gospel, without scandal to the community.

The distinction

This let me note in passing, this is the distinction between *some* accommodation for divorced pastors and *no* accommodation for sexually active homosexual pastors.

It isn't merely the quality of repentance we should seek to examine, but the evidence for it. How do we react to a divorced, remarried pastor who would say in the very first instance, there is nothing about his or her divorce for which repentance is needed? Marital disorder among clergy is not an argument for gay blessings. To the contrary, it is an argument against them.

I don't know if I have dealt with the theology adequately. Possibly, I have not. According to a friendly detractor, I am no theologian at all. I am a "mere journalist with theological pretensions." Like, I didn't know that. But what I have written here comes with eleven years of experience with divorce, my own struggles with being divorced, and I submit it to you.

Toward a practice of Christian divorce

I will now make some modest suggestions to the church. The progression I noted earlier went from immediate resignation, to bishops and district presidents examining the exigencies of a particular divorce on an individual case-by-case basis, to a now rather general blanket disregard. I do not think we are the better for it.

This is a note I received from a long acquaintance, a former pastor no longer on the clergy roster. He now teaches religion and philosophy at a southern state university. To his great embarrassment, he has been divorced and remarried three times. He says,

> Personally, I feel I have not been done any favors by [the ELCA's] easy-going attitude toward divorce, even though I am glad that I got to be a parish pastor, and think I did okay at it. At the very least there could have been a lot more severity. Instead, nobody in the church said "boo." It might have saved me a lot of suffering and confusion if someone had pulled me aside at the right moment (or at any moment), opened the New Testament, and said, "Look here. Now just what are you contemplating?"[11]

Bishops are the ones to ask these questions. I believe we must ask bishops and pastors, like it or not, to again approach these matters on a case-by-case examination. I believe we must ask divorcing pastors to justify their divorce because I have met too many pastors, and so have you, who flaunt their divorce as a "creative growth experience." I have heard from and about those who claim their complete innocence, and I have known those who parade their innocence in a bid for sympathy. I have met those who angrily contend it is entirely a private matter, and nobody else's business but their own.

These examples all too much reflect our culture. On issues of marriage and divorce, the church has stumbled into "no fault" along with the culture, and we have made a botch of it. The church may, must, both endure and engage the culture around us, but we should not do so as "those who have no hope." [12]

This will sound very odd, I know, but if we cannot eliminate divorce, we must "Christianize" it. We must develop a practice of Christian divorce, and we must apply it first to our ministerium.

Justifying continued service

When I said that pastors should be expected to justify their divorce, I really mean they should justify their continued service in the ordained ministry. The presumption should be for the pastor's immediate leave from call, a self-paid sabbatical, and it is an expectation that both bishop and pastor should carry, mindful there may be possible exceptions, perhaps many possible exceptions. But the first presumption should be, leave from call. The pastor should offer it, and the bishop should think about accepting it.

And while the bishop is thinking about it, there are questions to be asked and expectations to be met and the bishop should ask the questions, and define the expectation. Foremost, pastor and spouse should be reminded that the Eighth Commandment remains in effect, even among divorcing Christians.

I would ask a whole array of privacy-invading questions. Who is filing for the divorce, and why? The bishop should insist on marital counseling, and he should expect to be able to speak with the counselor directly.

There ought to be other questions, too. What are the provisions for dividing marital assets? What provision for the children and visitation? Why do you, pastor, want to remain in this parish when your ex-spouse is moving 1,000 miles away with the children? And you, ex-spouse, why is it you want to remove the children from the other parent? All of the issues in divorce should be examined, with a view to assessing the pastor's continued fitness for public ministry.

I also think the church should put in place "safe harbors" for mediation and arbitration for divorcing Christians, especially for divorcing pastors and their spouses. These services ought to be available as an alternative to an adversarial legal system that puts people at each other's throats, whether they intend it or not.

I know Lutherans are very uncomfortable with prescriptions for behavior. "Works righteousness" still sends shivers up Lutheran spines. But what, realistically, becomes of the church when all sorts of clergy sins get treated as inconsequential? Eventually, all sin becomes inconsequential. If we cannot take care with divorcing clergy, what other areas of behavior must also go unchallenged?

It is crucial to understand that here in the midst of real life our faith is interwoven with our ethics, our behavior. There is a necessary connection between what we say and what we do. The suggestions I have made are not to find fault, nor assign blame. Yet if the questions I raise are honestly asked and honestly answered, the answer of what to do—case by case—will become apparent.

The alternative is what we presently have.

Russell E. Saltzman is pastor of Ruskin Heights Lutheran Church, Kansas City, Missouri and editor of Forum Letter, *published by the American Lutheran Publicity Bureau. His articles have appeared in* The Lutheran, Lutheran Partners, First Things, The Christian Century, *and in many other publications.*

[1] Conference on Christian Sexuality, October 24-26, Kansas City, Missouri

[2] *Interpreter's Dictionary of the Bible* Vol. I, page 859

[3] Teachings and Practice on Marriage, Divorce, and Remarriage, American Lutheran Church Statement, adopted September 10, 1983

[4] *cf.* Arthur Carl Piepkorn, "The Doctrine of Marriage in the Theologians of Lutheran Orthodoxy," *Concordia Theological Monthly*, XXIV, 1953

[5] *cf.* Russell E. Saltzman, "Toward a Liturgical Ethic for Marriage," *Lutheran Forum*, Advent 1981

[6] *Lutheran Book of Worship*, p. 203

[7] *Visions and Expectations: Ordained Ministers in the ELCA*; adopted October 1990, Evangelical Lutheran Church in America

[8] "Mighty Fall," Martin E. Marty, *Christian Century*:119:21

[9] *The Ninety-Five Theses* by Martin Luther

[10] Psalm 51:18

[11] Private correspondence

[12] *cf.* First Thessalonians 4:13

✖ Chapter Five

Ritualizing Life or Ritualizing Death

By Amy C. Schifrin

When I ask a pastor, any pastor, "What would you prefer; a wedding or a funeral?" the unanimous response is, "A funeral, of course!" No wedding coordinators, no matching tangerine bridesmaids gowns, no swooping soloists, no ten-gallon hats, no melting unity candles, no mother of the bride and (even more adamantly!) no pouting mother of the groom, no Wagnerian overtones, no diaper-wearing ring-bearers, and most of all no folks who could care less about the life of fidelity that our Lord calls us to lead. "Give me a 'good' funeral any day," they say. At a funeral there is one thing to be said and just about everybody knows they need to hear it.

It is a multi-billion dollar industry, this wedding stuff. Whether one understands it sacramentally, or as a matter of civic order, or somewhere in-between, it's pretty hard not to get caught up in the frou-frou. Yet weddings remain one of the centerpieces of our culture.

Ritualizing what cannot be said
In ancient times, marriage was often by capture; in the days of Jesus it was most likely by purchase; and in the aftermath of the romanticizing tendencies of the twelfth century, it is now, in the West, said to be a matter of mutual consent. Sure, folks have just lived together without the aid of a preacher's blessing, and certainly folks have copulated together without the preacher's blessing; but in spite of that most folks have sought a ritual to express something about this union that they could find no other way to express. That's the thing about ritualizing: whether with straightforward vows and an exchange of rings in the

judge's chambers, or with twelve blushing bridesmaids and four-hundred well-heeled guests, people have sought to say through their ritualizing what they could not say in any other way. Besides everything else they are, weddings function as a major symbol in our culture, and thus they reflect our understanding of material reality, as well as point beyond themselves to meanings rich, deep, and often ultimate. Rituals call us to pay attention, and by their repetition they draw us ever-again into new depths of meaning. Such public patterning is a source of power that is never neutral.

What we learn from weddings is that in the beginning God made them male and female, and that procreation, delight, complimentarity, and community are rolled into this pairing. We find, through the symbolic acts of this marriage rite, ways to express what we hope this union to be and to become. Like many symbolic acts, these slowly change as what we're seeking to express changes. There is no longer a provision in the *Lutheran Book of Worship* for the ancient question, "Who gives this woman to be with this man?" because the understanding of woman as property is beginning to change. I say "beginning," because countless young brides still have their fathers escort them down the aisle and place their hand on their intended's arm after the two men have shaken hands. The ritualized, deeply patterned gestures speak the question in a far more authoritative voice than the words ever could have done.

Marriage is a classic rite of passage. Whether as an exchange of property or an expression of consent, and regardless of whether we speak of it as a sacrament or a civil estate, getting married is the clearest way our society knows to mark the completion of the transition from childhood into adulthood. Something changes in the way that we are perceived by society. We hope something also changes in the way that we live and place our energies. At the onset of adolescence there are tribal and often ecclesiastical rites to mark the maturing body and mind, but marriage, which signifies the end of adolescence, marks one as an adult in a way that nothing else can. "Therefore a man leaves his father and mother and is joined to his wife." Such an announcement is both prescriptive and descriptive as the Creator's intention in joining together that particular woman and that particular man is sealed. It is a rite that sanctifies life, that is, it not only announces the goodness of the Creator's intentions; it also gives us a means to live out his delight. [1]

Yet even as this rite of passage sanctifies life, the church has retained many of the ancient pagan customs for this rite. These include everything from rings on the fourth finger, bridal veils, and floral crowns to wedding banquets and the carrying of the bride over the threshold. [2]

The church has also held differing rationales as to how it is to function and/or regulate this rite, as well as its ecclesiastical and societal consequences. Unfortunately, regardless of what we Christians may think, people who have no intention of living as devoted disciples and participating in the on-going life of a particular ecclesiastical community "rent" our sanctuaries for "their" rituals. In such instances marriage is not the place to celebrate the fidelity of God toward us in our life-long fidelity toward each other; rather people now come to ritualize their love for each other — and the stained glass windows make such a nice backdrop. Heaven forbid that the paraments clash with the bridesmaids' gowns!

Why not same-sex blessings

In line with this current generation's idea of a wedding being "the public expression of a loving commitment," voices have arisen demanding that the church publicly bless the relationships of same-sexed persons who express their own "loving commitment" homoerotically.[3] "Why not" they ask? "We were born that way. We have a right to the same protection as everyone else; we have a right to be considered adults."[4] Underlying all the other reasons that the church should not bless the living out of homoerotic desires is the basic understanding of what is being ritualized in this rite of passage. Homoeroticism does not signify adult behavior; in fact it is expressive of a developmental truncation as it locks one into one of those great stages of development that adolescents are called to move through on their way to maturity. Single people, however they express their erotic affections, have no public marker of adult acceptance. Graduation from college or from boot camp is significant but these are tied to action, not being. No other rites of passage suffice, with the exception of vows of profession of religious women and the ordination of Roman Catholic priests, where a sexual component, here defined celibately, is made public.

So now there are voices within the church asking for a ritualizing of same-gender committed homoerotic relationships. What other way can folks whose current affections are homoerotic truly be adults in this society? But what if such relationships are at a developmental impasse? Do we want to lock folks into the perpetual angst of early adolescence? Weddings, which both mirror and ritualize the Creator's intent in design, are patterns that we create to mark the completion of the transition to mature adulthood.[5] Such rituals say that spirituality and sexuality are closely entwined. They say that one of the ways we come to know God's love is by loving one who is *other* than ourselves. They say that this attraction was built into God's intention for our lives, and that it is good. They say that this pairing is for the betterment of society as it intends for children to have the constancy and protection of both a male and a female parent. Such ritualizing says most significantly, "Lord Jesus Christ, as you freely give yourself to your bride the Church, grant that the mystery of the union of man and woman in marriage may reveal to the world the self-giving love which you have for your church; and to you with the Father and the Holy Spirit be glory and honor now and forever."[6] Narcissism be gone: the substance and display of their love is for the sake of world, not for the self, and not only for each other.[7]

Is the church willing to say that about homoerotic relationships? Do homoerotic relationships allow for the radical transformation that comes from learning to love one who is truly other than oneself? Or in homoeroticism does one simply meet oneself—untransformed—again and again? Are homoerotic relationships for the sake of the world? It has been my experience as a parish pastor that they are not. Let me speak first about my experience in working with women.

As a female pastor, I have often had women come in for counseling who were sexually abused. Like every other pastor, male or female, I have spoken with many people who come from all sorts of discouraging and abusive familial contexts; but for this conversation I want to focus on the sexual dimensions, whether the abuse was physical or emotional—both of which, of course, are spiritually diminishing.

Time and time again I have had women speak to me about their participation (or former participation) in lesbian relationships. Within their histories I would hear the refrains of insecurity, rejection, abandonment, abuse, and occasionally torture. Fear of penetration in a woman whose body was penetrated brutally is a temporary means of survival, which now has become its own deadly prison. Something was stolen from these women, something beautiful and something holy: their femininity, which was made to reflect their Creator's glory. Some man set himself up as a god with the power of life and death over them, and now they have locked the gate for fear that what is left of their being will be taken from them. If the church were to proclaim, "God made you this way," our action would give more power to the perpetrators who robbed these women of their birthright.

In other cases the women who seek their solace in lesbian affections are those who were robbed of nurture by mothers who did not accept or love their own femininity. Still other women are simply physically built to be the antithesis of the Barbie doll, and they have only known the taunts of boys and the distancing of men.[8] It's easy to see how a young woman with those physical characteristics and emotional deficits would say as an adult that she always thought of herself as different, that she had always been a lesbian. She has always been rejected by men and in her now "butch" demeanor, she will "set up a situation in which she…has to be rejected, or defend against the possibility by being the first to reject."[9] Providing a ritual that would then lock her into what should be at most a transitory/developmental phase would be totally lacking in compassion. It is the easy answer to give to a woman who is hurting. It is much more difficult to walk with her in her pain; not knowing when healing will come but just knowing its cruciform shape. If we lock her into a homoerotic "identity" because she simply needs to find security in the company of another woman before she can find security in herself,[10] then we have done her a great disservice. We have taken away the possibility of healing under the guise of sexual identity. I believe that it is far better to find that security in the sort of companionship and mentoring that does not transgress one's sexual boundaries, especially for young vulnerable women whose patterns of affection are just being formed.

A Berkeley vignette

In the cultural situation in which we find ourselves at the start of this new century, children and adolescents are taught in some public schools that "you were born this way." Let me place a vignette before you, a real story that takes place in Berkeley, California, 2001 – 2002. Two girls begin their freshman year at Berkeley High School. Like all freshman at Berkeley High, they are required to take Freshman Core, which consists of two courses, English, and Identity & Ethnic Studies. The first required book that both girls will read in Freshman Core is *Coffee Will Make You Black*, the sexually explicit coming-out story of a black lesbian.[11] During the course of the school year both their English teacher and their Identity & Ethnic Studies teachers will "come out" to them as self-identified homosexuals, one as a gay man, the other as a lesbian. In addition, their curriculum will include a variety of guest speakers who are self-identified gays, lesbians, and bisexuals who will advocate for the normalizing of such identities into society.

Now both of these girls are fourteen. Both of them are short, both of them have unkempt hair, both of them are lacking in simple social skills, both of them wear big baggy cloths over their developing yet overweight bodies, and by mid-spring, both of them begin to wonder if they are bisexual. Boys seem to prefer the girls who look like Brittany Spears, so maybe they weren't meant to be in relationships with boys. They cling to each other as a safe harbor against all the changes around them and in them, against all those other girls who seem to be moving on towards young adulthood, against all those boys who have teased them about being fat or unattractive. For a wide variety of reasons they simply do not have the internal resources to take the next developmental step, and now they've learned that there isn't another step to take.

If, seven or eight years down the road, they decide to make a commitment to one who is their mirror image, how could the church ritualize that? How could the church bless that? Would it be good for the sake of the world to bless such a union? Frankly, it would be cruel and hateful to all generations of young women and young men yet to come. Since the American Psychiatric Association's politicized declassification of homosexuality as a disorder twenty years ago, the church needs to be the voice of hope, calling into question yet another human folly.[13]

The word that we mostly receive from the media these days is that sexual identity is only a matter of your DNA. The gay/lesbian/bisexual/transgendered (hereafter GLBT) lobby knows that there is far more to it, but they also know that the quickest way to get the general populace to support them is to claim that it is solely genetic, for then how could one disagree? The argument they places before us is, "How could the church not bless such unions if they are biologically predetermined, if they are a matter of living out God's intention for a person whose affections have always been toward a member of the same gender?"

Self-degradation

So now let of turn for a moment to male homoerotic behaviors and ask if they sanctify life and how the church might ritualize these pairings. Just as sexual expression blossoms between a wife and a husband leading to a lovemaking that includes intercourse, erotic expression between two men leads to anal sex. One man's penis is thrust into another man's anus. That which is capable of bearing life is inserted into the place of decay and death. Just as a young women seeks the missing maternal from the body of another woman, here a man seeks to the missing masculine as he penetrates another man. His need for unconditional male love that is necessary for growth into mature manhood comes at the cost of self-degradation as it is sexualized through male-male intercourse. Having anal intercourse with another man will not give him that which he needs to grow into a mature man, and through the particularities of the homoerotic physical encounter he will be diminished even more. This is reinforced when he is on the receiving end, for the domination of another man is internalized and the maleness given in God's image to all men is perverted in his body. Unlike Herbert

Chilstrom and Lowell Erdahl, I can find no aspect of this physical encounter that is "life-giving."[14]

All of us have masculine and feminine dimensions to our personalities, but have you ever noticed the caricature of women by men who engage in sexual acts with other men? Femininity is camped up, but it always carries the male distortion of the feminine in its expression. An effeminate "gay" man really isn't like a woman and so his actions and demeanor are like a reflection in a carnival mirror where certain aspects of femininity are blown out of proportion while others are masked. Despite his allowing another man to penetrate him, he is still a man, not a woman, and his body was not made with a womb that receives and returns life with joy. What are two men seeking in asking the church to bless a relationship that expresses itself in an erotic behavior that is diminishing to both of them, that takes life away from both of them? With wisdom and with compassion the church needs to respond in a way that helps them move away from such behaviors to a place where they can find a true male identity, an identity that gives them the resources and courage to love one who is truly other, that is, a woman, and in so doing they will at last receive their own masculinity as a gift. If two men stand in tuxes, hold hands, and profess their love for one another while a pastor announces to a gathered congregation that they are now a couple in the sight of God, the church's ritualizing of the sanctity of life becomes now a pseudo-sanctity, a false witness which is detrimental to those men as well as destructive to our understanding of marriage.

Like for gay people

Let me share a small example of how the blessing of same-sex unions will continue to erode the understanding of marriage as that which takes place for the sake of the world. Recently I received a phone call from a woman who is living with a man whom she names as her fiancée. She called to see if I would "do" a marriage ceremony for them that wasn't really a legal marriage. They want it to look and sound like a marriage, but they don't want to be legally married because he would lose money from a trust fund. But they *do* love each other and they are *committed* to each other, she said. After a lengthy discussion, I said that I would be glad to meet with them and discuss their situation, but I wanted them to know that I would not marry them without a wedding license nor would I engage deception for the sake of their families. She said to me, "I just want a commitment ceremony, you know, like you do for gay people." "I don't do those either," I responded, and was reminded once again that all rites are interlocking.

How we as a church enact God's grace in a Baptism service is related to how we enact it in a Eucharistic service, or at a wedding, or at a funeral, or at ordination. This leads us to the second half of this discussion of ritualization as we consider ordination. How the church handles same-sex homoerotic relations is directly related to how the church will handle the request for the ordination of open and active self-identified gays, lesbians, bisexuals and transgendered persons.

The public ministry of the baptized

All baptized Christians are called to faithful ministry. This chosen race, this royal priesthood, this holy nation: the baptized are called into great ministries where in thought, word, and deed they are to live out the goodness, mercy, and fidelity of God. Within the priesthood of the baptized, there are those women and men called to the public ministry of word and sacrament, and through the work of the Spirit they are sent to many and varied congregations. Candidacy committees, supportive parishes, seminary faculty, and sometimes a bishop's hands are involved in saying, "Feed my sheep." But who should be sent out? Are there behaviors that are unacceptable for those in public ministry? Who decides, and by what criteria? As part of our ritual strategy we ask, "Will you...preach and teach in accordance with the Holy Scripture...the [historic creeds] and [the Lutheran] confessions? ...Will you...nourish God's people with the Word and Holy Sacraments, and lead them by your own example in faithful service and holy living? Will you give faithful witness in the world, that's God's love may be known in all that you do?"[15] At the heart of the ordinand's answer is a promise to preach and teach in accordance with the Scriptures and confessions and, as the *Church Book* once said, "to adorn the doctrine of our Savior by a holy life and godly conversation." We see from the GLBT agenda that one's hermeneutical guides for this promise can vary widely.

Who the church will ordain is as important symbolically as whom the church will marry. How the church makes its decisions as to who may be called has varied throughout the course of the church's history.

Women's ordination

Let us now take some time to examine the issue of the ordination of women, for here is a place where changes have occurred in the last century. I believe that the arguments and contexts, both pro and con, will be instructive for our discussion of GLBT ordination.

Were there women called into preaching and sacramental ministries in the earliest decades of the church? Are there unanimous or differing voices in Scripture as to women's roles in the life of the community? Do we have any evidence of women's leadership and/or subordination in ways that would inform our current notions of public sacramental ministry? Why, in 1970, did The American Lutheran Church and the Lutheran Church in America deem it right and salutary to call women to serve in ordained ministry? Why did that happen almost a century earlier among "non-sacramental" churches? Why has it not happened in the Roman Catholic Church? Lutheran biblical scholars examined the Scriptures some thirty years ago, and in that prayerful examination they came to believe that there was nothing in Scripture that forbids the ordination of women who promise to teach and preach in accordance with Scripture and the confessions, as well as lead a godly life.

Like all denominations that have struggled with the issue of women's ordination, they had to make some hermeneutical choices. How do we balance 1 Timothy 2:11-12 and 1 Corinthians 14.33b-35 on the one hand, and Galatians 3.28, 1 Corinthians 11.4-5, and Acts 2.16-18 on the other? As all these passages and many others were laid out within the context of Scripture interpreting Scripture, a decision was made in the affirmative for women. It was seen that they were part of that early apostolic community and they were indeed called to feed the sheep. Among these women were Euodia and Syntyche in Philippi (Philippians 4.2-3); Phoebe in Cenchare and Rome (Romans 16.1-2); Prisca, who with her husband Aquila had connections in Ephesus, Corinth and Rome (Romans 16.3; 1 Corinthians 16.19; Acts 18.2-28); and just to knock your socks off, there is Paul's greeting of Junia (Romans 16.7), a female apostle! Women began to be excluded from leadership when the church moved from house settings to basilicas, and the standards of Roman society prevailed.[16] As liturgy grew increasingly ocular in the following centuries, the maleness of the priest, as one who is called to re-present Christ at the altar, continued to hold sway even among many who moved far from Rome.[17] This is part of the reason why women in "non-sacramental" denominations were ordained decades before those in denominations whose celebration of the sacrament of the altar was held on par with the preaching of the word.[18] From a ritual studies perspective, one could even say that the use of men only as priests contributes to the formation of the doctrine of *in persona Christi*, for by restricting through practice what could be expressed such maleness is formalized as normative. And, of course, as long as a man took a vow of celibacy the question of "orientation" was irrelevant.[19]

While Lutherans held no official position with regards to Rome's continuing iconic argument, in practice they had enacted it for centuries. And so as the sacramental Reformation denominations moved to ordain women in the 1970s, Rome needed to make its position explicit and did so with the 1976 *Declaration on the Question of the Admission of Women to the Ministerial Priesthood*. This document insisted that "the Christian priesthood is therefore of a sacramental nature: the priest being a sign, the supernatural effectiveness of which comes from the ordination received, but a sign which must be perceptible and which the faithful must recognize with ease... [W]hen Christ's role in the Eucharist is to be expressed sacramentally, there would not be this 'natural resemblance' which must exist between Christ and his minister if the role of Christ were not taken by a man."[20] Pope John Paul II repeated and expanded this argument by declaring, "If Christ—by his free and sovereign choice, clearly attested to by the gospel and by the church's constant tradition—entrusted only to men the task of being an 'icon' of his countenance as 'shepherd' and 'bridegroom' of the church through the exercises of the ministerial priesthood, this in no way detracts from the role of women.'[21] In sacramental churches the inerrancy argument is masked and interpreted within the tradition.

A right to the rite

In the last half of the twentieth century, the lives of women in the western world changed drastically. During that time there were forces both within and without of the church calling for change for women as a matter of "justice" or (I would say) "entitlement." This is where the comparisons with GLBT agenda come into focus and this is the place where women clergy are so often co-opted by the GLBT movement. I am convinced that the ordination of women differs from that of sexually active GLBT persons on biblical and theological grounds. But if women understand their "right" to be ordained as a matter of social justice rather than as a mandate which comes from the ancient breath of the Spirit through the church; if women mistakenly believe that the church's move to ordain women is based on the principle of gender equity rather than on the precedent of biblical women preachers, then they have no way to oppose the GLBT agenda without being accused of hypocrisy. The similarities between ordination of women and ordination of sexually active GLBT persons come in the sociological realm as particular social movements have exercised political pressure on the church. This allows the proponents of the GLBT agenda to propagate a hermeneutic which says that all gender and sexuality issues are contextual. In so doing they gain the support of certain feminist women and men who now dismiss all those difficult verses of Scripture with a broad stroke.

Female or male, the pastor or priest as icon is polysemous to say the least, for in addition to any symbolic role within a denomination, she or he also carries a symbolic role to the world. The argument against ordaining women differs, of course, between those sacramental churches that believe that women are not able to represent Christ and the inerrantist denominations whose selective literalism leads them to focus primarily on the submission of women to men.[22] It is important to note that Baptists in this country began ordaining women as early as 1895, but by the mid-twentieth century had rescinded that permission as their inerrancy grew more rigid. Their hermeneutic centered on their understanding of the passages from 1 Timothy 2 and 1 Corinthians 14, and they used those verses as the guide through which they filtered the other scriptural passages. Other inerrantist communities used Galatians 3.28, 1 Corinthians 11.4-5 and Acts 2.16-18 as their hermeneutical guide and found ordaining women to be consistent with their inerrancy. It appears that the Scriptures could be made to bend according to the particular social context. It is the social context now that surrounds the issue of GLBT ordination, for the scriptural witness in this case is without the ambiguity that is present in the debate concerning women. The scriptural witness with regard to GLBT ordination is a unified "no." But if the church sets Scripture aside and uses social context as its primary hermeneutical guide, then Scripture, which knows nothing of "orientation," can more easily be dismissed as not having a legitimate voice in the conversation.

How does a denomination get itself into such a conundrum? As with the issue of the ordination of women, there are pressures from the greater society which are now advocated for by people within the denomination.[23] Sociologist of religion Mark Chavez, asserts that the changing social understanding of women is more significant that how one understands Scripture as an impetus toward the ordination of women.[24] Chavez's research also points to autonomous women's organizations within a denomination and how centralized a denomination is as major catalysts for change even without pressure from individual women seeking ordination.[25] Whether or not there were female candidates lining up at the seminaries, the ordination of women gave a signal to the wider ecumenical community and to the world as to where a church body positioned itself on the theological-political spectrum.

So now let us ask, will the pressures that come from autonomous GLBT advocacy groups within the ELCA such as Lutherans Concerned serve as the hermeneutical catalyst for the ordination of open and active self-identified gays, lesbians, bi-sexual, and trans-gendered persons? What happens to a church body when seminaries admit to their pastoral degree programs individuals who are openly pursing homo-erotic relationships? What happens when candidacy committees affirm self-identified sexually active GLBT persons? What happens when bishops mistake self-destructive behavior for love and allow those who are engaged in homoerotic activity to join or remain on the clergy roster so long as that activity occurs within a "committed relationship"? GLBT ordination and blessing same-sex committed relationships is a seamless garment. Martin Luther once had to deal with the interconnectedness of spirituality and sexuality when celibate priests became married pastors. So now if the church decides to ordain open and active GLBT persons, the church will have to deal with provisions for all sorts of familial relationships.

For the sake of the world

Pastors are human beings — and as a church body we celebrate when a pastor has a healthy, life-affirming marriage. Not only is such a marriage a blessing to his or her spouse and to their children (if they are blessed with children), but for the congregation as well as they look to their pastor as one among them who promised to give "faithful witness in the world, that God's love would be known in all that [they] do."[26] All that we are called to do is for the sake of the world, because from the beginning, all that we were called to be was for the sake of the world, too.

Amy C. Schifrin is pastor of Bethlehem Lutheran Church, St. Cloud, Minnesota. She is the former seminary pastor at Pacific Lutheran Theological Seminary, Berkeley, California, and is completing her doctoral program at the Graduate Theological Union in Berkeley.

---

[1] "The attempt to make a set of activities appear to be identical to or thoroughly consistent with older cultural precedents can be called 'traditionalization.' As a powerful tool of legitimation, traditionalization may be the near-perfect repetition of activities from an earlier period, the adaptation of such activities in a new setting, or even the creation of practices that simply evoke links with the past... A ritual that evokes no connection with any tradition is apt to be found anomalous, inauthentic, or unsatisfying by most people." Catherine Bell, *Ritual: Perspectives and Dimensions* (New York and Oxford: Oxford University Press, 1997), 145.

[2] Frank Senn, *Christian Liturgy: Catholic and Evangelical* (Minneapolis: Fortress Press, 1997), 167.

[3] Ibid., 666.

[4] Type "holy unions" in your search engine and you will discover the glamour, glitz, and politically correct romance of gay and lesbian commitment services.

[5] "By means of ritual, relationship to the unchanging archetypal aspects of existence was affirmed and renewed." Marion Woodman, *The Pregnant Virgin: A Process of Psychological Transformation* (Toronto: Inner City books, 1985), 18.

[6] Post-Communion Prayer for the Rite of Marriage, *Lutheran Book of Worship Minister's Desk Edition*, (Minneapolis and Philadelphia: Augsburg Publishing and Board of Publications, Lutheran Church in America, 1978), 192. See also Revelation 19.7; Ephesians 5.25.

[7] Philip Pfatteicher, *Commentary on the Occasional Services* (Philadelphia: Fortress Press, 1983), 469.

[8] "A woman whose mother did not love her own femininity, and who therefore rejected the female body of her daughter, almost inevitably goes through a period of lesbian dreams or lesbian acting out because her body requires the acceptance of a woman." Woodman, 59.

[9] Ibid., 109.

[10] Ibid., 38.

[11] April Sinclair, *Coffee Will Make You Black* (New York: Avon Books, 1994).

[12] "Being gay is as natural, normal, and healthy as being straight." "Be yourself: Questions and Answers for Gay, Lesbian, and Bisexual Youth" (Washington, DC: PFLAG, 1999), 4.

[13] The way for this move was paved internally by closeted gay psychiatrists, who, if their behavior had been known, would not have been allowed to enter this profession pre-1973.

[14] Herbert W. Chilstrom and Lowell O. Erdahl, *Sexual Fulfillment for Single and Married, Straight and Gay, Young and Old* (Minneapolis: Augsburg Press, 2001).

[15] *Occasional Services: A Companion to the Lutheran Book of Worship* (Minneapolis and Philadelphia: Augsburg Publishing House and Board of Publication, Lutheran Church in America, 1982), 194.

[16] Karen Jo Torjesen, *When Women Were Priests* (San Francisco: Harper, 1995), 155-172.

[17] The church's exclusive use of male priests, like the scholastic canon of the mass, its Eucharistic gestural fundamentalism, and its use of relics are all ways that it tried to bring a dead body to life.

[18] Mark Chavez, *Ordaining Women: Culture and Conflict in Religious Organizations* (Cambridge, Massachusetts and London: Harvard University Press, 1997), 85.

[19] Of course the arguments against ordaining women take on a different tone based on a church's sacramentalist or inerrantist leanings. In the case of GLBT ordination among fundamentalist Protestants, the arguments are not sacramental but scriptural.

[20] Sacred Congregation for the Doctrine of the Faith (1976); cited in Chavez, 87.

[21] Ibid., 87-88.

[22] Ibid. 90.

[23] Chavez argues that the meanings of women's ordination changes when it is framed by the gender equity issues of the women's movement. Chavez, 75.

[24] Ibid., 49.

[25] Ibid., 142-157.

[26] *Occasional Service Book*, 194.

Chapter Six

**The Spiritual Nature and Destiny of the Human Body:
A Pastoral Perspective on Human Sexuality**

By Phillip Max Johnson

I am asked to address the current contentious questions about human sexuality from a "pastoral perspective." To remind myself what that perspective is I return to the vows spoken when I assumed the pastoral office "before almighty God, to whom [I] must give account." There I am reminded that the pastoral perspective is that of the biblical exegete and theologian, since I have promised to be diligent in my study of the Scriptures (and since, after all, the gathered Christian community is the center and goal of theology and exegesis). I find in the vows that my perspective will be ecumenical, catholic and confessional, as I have sworn to teach according to the ecumenical creeds and Lutheran confessions. My perspective, then, will be that of preacher and catechist. As a steward of the mysteries, my perspective will be liturgical and sacramental. Finally, it will be deeply personal and penitential, having been called to lead God's people by the example of holy living, and "so that after proclaiming to others I myself should not be disqualified" (1 Corinthians 9:27). In and through all this, my perspective will be determined by the stunning gospel promise that rests upon the congregation.

Mediated care

The ordination vows determine the perspective, and also the pastoral care I am authorized and empowered to offer. Pastoral care is not, after all, some discrete activity among others in the pastor's work. Pastoral care is simply what I am called to do in and through accurate exegesis, faithful theological reflection, preaching the law and gospel of God, administering the sacraments, hearing confessions, providing spiritual direction or encouragement or warning, praying ceaselessly with and for God's people, and seeking out the sick, the weak, the troubled, and the indifferent to extend this holy ministry to them.

This is a particular vocation in the Church and in the world. In disorienting times I have found it necessary to remind myself of its particularity, and also of its limitations. If the care I am offering a person or congregation is not *this* care, it may be called "care," maybe even "Christian care," it may be offered caringly, but it is not pastoral care in the gospel-specific sense, as outlined by my ordination.

I have learned from Dietrich Bonhoeffer to conceive of this as *mediated* care.[1] My relationship to those whom I am called to serve is an entirely mediated relationship — mediated by Christ, that is, by the Word and the sacraments, and by prayer. Just so, it is always a liturgically structured relationship, even if the appropriate liturgy may be very subtly enacted at the bedside or over a coffee table. Does this preclude intimacy and deep personal sympathy? On the contrary, it is the depth of pastoral intimacy that makes it so important that the liturgy be in place.

From this pastoral perspective I see an *end* to this caring labor. The end of pastoral care is freedom from sin and death, a freedom towards which my pastoral work tends as an enacted prayer, "Come, Lord Jesus," but which even now may be tasted in the life of the faithful in the care provided. The end is the free service of God, maturity in Christ's new humanity, life eternal. So it is that *this* "caring profession" is defined by its faith profession. It is not defined by the various life projects and goals of individual Christians, or by the program goals that come and go in denominational life, or by my own anxieties about being useful. *Christian pastoral care is offered entirely by faith and not by the works of the caring personality* with its elastic and unpredictable (and sometime self-serving) sympathies. Faith clings to the *end* as our true heritage, divinely promised and divinely assured.

This promised end not only differentiates pastoral care from other kinds of care (such as medical or psychotherapeutic care, or the professional's care for a client, or a friend's care for a friend). It may, in certain instances, place pastoral care in conflict and competition with what many people think it means to be "caring." For example, generally speaking, if you care about others you care very much about their peace of mind; you want to be supportive in their bid for happiness. Sin being what it is, however, the kingdom of peace of mind and the Kingdom of God are not *yet* synonymous. Faithful care may require that I strive to do the unhappy work of seeking to undermine the peace of mind of a Christian (or the congregation) in order to agitate on behalf of the competing gospel end – if, for example, I am called to exercise such care among the indolent rich, or towards the man who wishes to abandon his wife because he is no longer in love with her, or in prayerful struggle with a Christian who has shaped an "identity" round his or her experienced sexual longings.

In this essay, I will come to speak about that *end* in terms of the gospel promises that rest upon the baptized bodies in the congregation before me. But let me first add a little personal history to my pastoral perspective on sexual ethics.

A Pastoral Time and Place

I have served almost entirely in inner city parishes in London or the metropolitan New York area. The county in which I serve is one of the most crowded on the continent, and one of the most ethnically diverse. We are, in Jersey City, a community of immigrants. My wife, my children and I love the place with it human richness. But there is much spiritual and physical ugliness, there are many poor people, and there is much suffering. We have the highest cases per capita of AIDS in the U.S. The congregation I serve reflects our place, with the good and the bad. Some 200 poor and homeless people come through our doors every month seeking help. Children from drug-ravaged families live in one of our houses. Every Sunday at the altar rail there will be at least one person dying of the AIDS virus. I have buried children shot in the head for no good reason, or who have frozen to death after fleeing a broken home, or who were slain in a high-speed car chase. More than one of my parishioners I first met by paying a visit to the county jail or the state prison.

Why do I speak of all this? Simply to indicate that in my pastoral perspective questions of sexual ethics and ethos are matters of life or death. No ethical issue is nearer the center where poverty, illness, crime, sickness, violence converge in social disintegration. This, of course, has always been true, and the truth is now much documented by the social sciences. But for some time the ethical revisionism of the Western elite culture – accessible to the young people in my neighborhood through the standard venues of popular culture (especially, as I have observed, in the sit-coms) – has been providing the ideological cover for the chaos in the now familiar slogans about sexual-identity, self-expression, personal authenticity, non-evaluative tolerance, and genetic determinism. Certain Christian denominations, the ones whose mostly white and well-to-do memberships owe their sense of legitimacy to the good opinion of Christianity's "cultured despisers," hurry along behind to work out the necessary theological-ethical amendments.

Given my experience of the ravages of what might be called a principled permissive sexual ethos upon those I serve, my pastoral perspective has indeed been focused by the now contentious issues of sexual ethics. Please notice I say refocused *by*, rather than refocused *on*.

What has my perspective been refocused *on*? — on the bodies of my parishioners. I have become intensely interested, pastorally and theologically, in the bodies of my parishioners. I have found myself needing to address the people as living bodies, to become more curious about the way they conceive their own bodies. I have had to remember their baptism as a bodily event and ask what that has to do with the wide continuum of bodily events that make up their lives. I have had to relearn the biblical focus on our shared bodily life and ponder aloud with the people the dignity and the destiny bestowed on their baptized bodies by the gospel.

What does this mean for my pastoral work and care? Very specifically:

1. As parish theologian, my perspective has been refocused on the doctrine of Creation and the relation of the Creation to the Redemption.
2. As parish preacher, it has been re-directed to the *one* Word of God as creating-commanding-redeeming. Indeed what has been called the "civic use of the law" has taken on a new importance in my perspective!
3. As parish exegete, my perspective has been riveted to the doctrine of the Body of Christ in its ethical implications.
4. As presiding minister in the liturgy, I have had tried to uncover the hidden theological connections between sacramental worship and sacramental sex.
5. As catechist and teacher I have had to try to make explicit the hidden connections in all of the above, to begin to see with my people the unified biblical vision of the *humanum*.

A darkening of vision

In saying that my perspective has been focused *by* rather than simply *on* the questions of sexual ethics, I express my conviction about the nature of our current crisis in the churches over the meaning and morals of sex. We misread the times, I think, if we see it only in terms of a "moral crisis" or an ethical argument. We wrongly discern the spirits if we ascribe our troubles to a cadre of ideologically driven revisionists who are now victimizing the churches from their places of political ascendancy. I know there are such people, they are just now pretty thick in the church bureaucratic offices, and they have a lot to answer for. But how their way was prepared, and how it is that there is so little and effective resistance among us to their initiatives, is a long story involving us all. Is it not the case that, on the issues of human sexuality, the meaning of marriage, the sanctity of life, we rank-and-file pastors and the people we serve are largely alienated from the biblical text itself and from the historic teaching of the church? Are we not caught in a fog of incomprehension?

There are, of course, many among our pastors and in our churches who still hold to a formal commitment to biblical authority. Their moral instincts warn them to try to hang on to certain traditional ethical prohibitions about, for example, homoerotic behavior. They know the proof texts. But the contextual theological glue is missing. The prohibitions no longer have that quality of co-inherence within a unified vision. The morals no longer imply the mystery.

From my pastoral perspective, then, I think I see, not simply confusion, not simply the need for better information, not only the loss of confidence in a traditional ethical code, but an unraveling of the fabric of the Christian mind, a kind of darkening of Christian vision in large sectors of the church.

The fading of Christian creatureliness

This brings me back to the bodies of the folks I serve. In this darkening of Christian vision, they do not see their own bodies, theologically speaking. And if they do not see their own bodies, they do not see the *first thing* about the Bible. They are alienated from that *first text*, where their bodies make a first theological appearance. They are alienated, then, from the first things of the creed and certainly from anything like Luther's elucidation in the Small Catechism: "I believe that God has created me (has given me and still preserves my body and soul: eyes, ears, and all limbs and senses)."[2] (But, as this is not an accusation but a pastoral lament, let me speak not of "they" but of "we".) I do not mean, of course, that we formally disbelieve these first things or that God's truth does not work graciously in defiance of explicit human incomprehension. But the language we have learned to speak and the thoughts we have learned to think about ourselves are not much permeated by these first things.

How did this happen? Here my reading of our theological history and my pastoral struggles connect directly. It is now a familiar history:

how it was that in modern (post-Enlightenment) protestant theology, dominated by an interlocking Liberalism and Pietism, the doctrine of creation lost its place of honor in the mind of the churches; how both the learned and the popular presentations of the Faith lost grasp of the foundational place of "Creation" in the Old and New Testaments (and, therefore, how the Old Testament was relegated to "background"), how the first article of the creed became a kind of insubstantial prologue to the second.[3]

But what I am interested in is the attendant loss to Christian piety and theological self-understanding (and, therefore, morals). The Anglican monk Lionel Thornton entitled this theological era "the fading out of Christian creatureliness."[4] By this phrase he meant that the implicit *sense* of creatureliness that had marked Christian piety from the time of the New Testament to the Reformation had been greatly dulled. For modern day Christians in the West, the *tacit awareness of self as creature of God* has been diminished under the force of a whole range of cultural and religious developments.

This loss of the creaturely sense means, in turn, that our understanding of the nature and destiny of the human person is cut off from the biblical and catholic vision of life. Theoretically, this can be described in terms of a double "dualism" or alienation. First, the biblically conceived unity of the human person with the rest of the created order, with what we call "the world of nature," is no longer clearly apprehended. Human beings are *either* the masters over nature to which they no longer belong, *or* they are simply one of natures more complicated products. In this conceptual nightmare, we can have *either* time *or* eternity; we dwell *either* with the angels *or* with the beasts. We have no real human place of our own.

Secondly, the created unity of the human person under God is lost in a false body-psyche dualism, so that the relation of the human body to human identity is constantly in flux. In certain fields of endeavor we are forced to think of the human being constituted simply as biological organism; in others (like religion) we wish to think of the real self as being "in there" somewhere, related to, but hardly constituted by, the body. In this vision, biological and spiritual existences are both acknowledged, but as ontological strangers.

In this complex of unspoken assumptions, the spiritual and moral significance of the human body gets demoted to second place, or even drops out of the picture. There is, of course, great emphasis in our popular culture just now on the body as a necessary *instrument* of the self's fulfillment. The turn to "wholeness" is in part a reaction to dualistic habits of thought. But, from the biblical point of view, this represents but another *humiliation* of the body in moral and spiritual terms.

Ethical pietism

Let me speak more concretely about the hints and signs of the "fading of Christian creatureliness" in piety and morals. I cannot here draw all the connecting lines, and the picture below is admittedly impressionist. But I trust you will recognize it.

Consider funerals. I am thinking about the well-intended but not-quite-Christian word of consolation you often hear as you stare into the coffin. "That's not really Mary, there in that casket." Am I wrong to see this as one sign among many of the loss of a vivid hope in the resurrection of the body with the inevitable hyper spiritualization of heaven, leaving the preacher a little embarrassed at the "naïve" biblical vision of heaven as the holy happy hour where God has laid on the feast of fat foods and well-aged wines (Isaiah 25:6)?

Consider how effectively our people seem sealed off from a truly bodily, sacramental piety. Even where the sacramental forms are maintained as occasions for deep personal devotion, even where liturgical renewal has taken root and where the catechism is repeated, it seems clear to me that pietistic assumptions reign (in both liberal and conservative circles, among many Roman Catholics as well as Protestants). The human relation to God is conceived and sought as a direct and unmediated "spiritual" one. Ask the confirmands, ask their parents, about their most deeply spiritual activity. You may have to listen a long while before you hear anything about water, bread, wine, spoken word, or hands on the head.

Consider the obvious wall of incomprehension between our people and the *Small Catechism*'s explanation of the article on creation, if large sectors of Lutheran Christians are unable to conceive of a child in the womb as a person. If I am truly convinced that the intentional destruction of the undeniably living human *body* (arms, legs, eyes, ears, heart, brain, etc.) is no longer conceived as the destruction of a person, then how am I to conceive any constituting status, or any spiritual significance, for my own bodily configuration and existence?

With regard to the morals and meaning of marriage, what of the readiness of Protestants to simply write-off the question of artificial contraception as a legitimately moral question? After all, only a couple of generations ago the question at least seemed obvious enough? What of the loss of the instinctive creaturely joy of childbirth as an act of *God's* creation through his human co-creators? How shall we account for the relatively new unreflective acceptance of the notion of an intentionally childless marriage?

What has happened to the sense of Christian creatureliness, that the members of our churches can work up little moral repugnance at the news of a suicide—plenty of pity, plenty of guilt, but little moral repugnance?

Finally, consider the talk about right and wrong, especially regarding human relationships: the radically reductive appeal to inward disposition, intention, and motive. In current moral jargon concerning the good and the bad of sexual relations, the bodily *form* of the action in and of itself has no ethical or spiritual standing. This is obviously the case for those who think there is nothing to choose, morally speaking, between homosexual or heterosexual relations as long as right motive and intention are in place ("committed relationship"). But what of the common assumption that within marriage itself "anything goes," as long as it is consensual and mutually pleasurable, so that marriage becomes a little private space for the legitimate exercise of lust? This thought seems a stranger to our minds, that their might be a created somatic "shape" or configuration to the act of a woman and a man by which they "know" one another—a configuration that in itself bears an "iconic" spiritual significance and by which alone the beautiful but rebellious creature Eros obeys her Maker.

Sacramental worship—sacramental sex

In the above examples, I have intentionally mixed piety and morals. I have tried to bring before your minds the picture of that confused Christian we might call the ethical pietist—who cannot conceive that bodily actions in and of themselves, whether at the altar rail or in the bedroom, have any spiritual significance, except what might be granted them by "inner" motive or intention. I have purposefully "confused" piety and morals, because in my mind and in my pulpit I mean to "decompartmentalize" ethics and worship, to rediscover how it is that the biblical ethic, articulated in the plain word of Scripture, coheres in the doctrines of creation, redemption, eschatology, and the sacraments.

After all, as the Decalogue teaches us, the ethical dignity of the human creature is not something apart from our liturgical and sacramental dignity. There is, after all, an "organic" connection between, for example, the command to keep the Sabbath and the prohibition of murder, between the forbidding of idols and the forbidding of adultery

(Ezekiel 16:5-32). From the divine side, so to speak, the connection may be stated this way: the Word that creates, the Word that commands and the Word that redeems is the Word of the One Lord. From the human side, we might say it this way: our *moral* struggle is but the herald of our created dignity and our destined glory, as that dignity is remembered and that destiny is proclaimed in the sacramental gathering. Therefore the highest *ethical* duty of the creature is fulfilled in this alone — that in the obedient offering of the sacrifice of thanksgiving, human beings are re-called to their place of dignity as the appointed priests and stewards of the created order, through which the whole creation gives praise to God.

This restoration of the human creature takes place under the creating-commanding-redeeming Word of God through the creaturely *communion of bodies with bodies*, as these bodies are presented as living sacrifices, which is their spiritual worship (Romans 12:1-3). Or, as I say to the confirmands, in the liturgy we learn how to behave as bodies before our God. For in the liturgy we associate with humble *creatures* – bread, wine, and water, for example. In the world and in the church these creatures obey their creator more readily and simply than we rebellious human creatures. And see what dignity these more humble creatures are given in the liturgy![5]

The dignity of the body

With this reference to Romans 12 about the presentation of our bodies as living sacrifices, with the connection between the body of the Christian and the sacramental body Christ, we come finally to the exegetical foundations for a Christian theology of the human body, and, therefore, to the foundations for pastoral guidance and care. In this brief space, all I can do is remind you of the prominence of this theme in Paul's writings and its centrality in his ethical-theological vision, how this theme dominates in what he has to say about marriage and sexual ethics, and how the concept of "body" in Paul's theology unites in his vision the creating and the redeeming work of God. In this brief but wide-ranging exegetical reflection, it will become clear how it is that in the Old and New Testaments the consistent repugnance at sexual disorder and sin — including homoerotic relations, adultery, fornication, permissive divorce and remarriage — is anything but occasional, time-bound, or theologically peripheral, but is thoroughly woven into the unified theological and christological vision that simply *is* the Bible's unity.

In present circumstances, the natural place to begin a meditation on the New Testament doctrine of the Body of Christ is 1 Corinthians 6: 15-20, as the apostle confronts sexual behavior in the congregation.

> Do you not know that your bodies are members of Christ? Should I therefore take the members of Christ and make them members of a prostitute? Never! Do you not know that who-ever is united to a prostitute becomes one body with her? For it is said, "The two shall be one flesh." Every [other] sin that a person commits is outside the body; but the fornicator sins against the body itself. Or do you not know that your body is a temple of the Holy Spirit within you, which you have from God, and that you are not your own? For you were bought with a price; therefore glorify God in your body.

Notice that this brief "ethical" text introduces all the aspects of the "Body of Christ" theme which will appear later in this epistle and else-where in the New Testament.

First, the word "members" anticipates the organic understanding of the church as Body of Christ in 1 Corinthians 12, where "all members of the body, though many, are one body" in Christ (v. 12). Secondly, the designation of the Christian's body as "a temple of the Holy Spirit" in 6:19 sends us again to chapter 12, to the baptismal *incorporation* of our bodies: "For in the one Spirit were we all baptized into the one body" (12:13). The sacramental reference, in turn, brings to mind the eucharis-tic Body in which believers commune in the breaking of bread and the cup of blessing, and so are constituted as the one Body of Christ (1 Corinthians 10:16, 17). Moreover the sacramental solidarity in the *bro-ken* body and shed blood is already anticipated in chapter 6 — "you are not your own. For you were bought with a price" (vv. 19, 20). With regard to both personal ethics (chapter 6) and communal worship (chap-ter 11), Paul is concerned that the violations he is addressing represent a profaning of and a failure to discern Christ's own body (6:15 and 11:29, respectively).

Throughout these texts, in which ethical, sacramental, and ecclesial concerns are wedded, the depth of the Spirit-given *organic union of the body of the believer with the risen body of Jesus* is profound in its "realism," bestowing high theological dignity upon the human body. Nor is such realism peculiar to 1 Corinthians. Elsewhere and often in the New Tes-tament, it appears in relation to the physical suffering of the believer. The most striking passage may stand for several others. In Colossians 1:22-24 once again the crucified and risen body of Jesus, his ecclesial body in the world, and the body of the Christian (in this case, the body of the apostle himself) are seen as organically unified in the redemptive vision. Paul addresses the church as those who were once estranged and hostile to God, but whom Christ "has now reconciled *in his fleshly body*, so as to present you holy and blameless and irreproachable before him." Then the apostle looks to his own role as servant of their redemption. "I am now rejoicing in my sufferings for your sake, and *in my flesh* I am completing what is lacking in Christ's afflictions for the sake of his body, that is, the church" (italics added). Such is the dignity of the baptized body, that even and especially its physical vulnerability may constitute bodily fellowship with the wounded and risen body of the incarnate Word.

The nature of the body

We may trace yet another connecting exegetical line emerging from 1 Corinthians 6, this time leading forward to Ephesians 5 and backward to Genesis 2. In both New Testament texts, Genesis 2:24 is quoted — "the two shall become one flesh." In Ephesians 5, as in 1 Corinthians 6, an immediate concern with Christian *behavior* opens out into the wider context of the redemptive history. "Husbands love your wives just as Christ loved the church and gave himself for her — so as to present the church to himself in splendor — so that she may be holy and without blemish" (vv. 25-27). The comparison continues with reference to the body. "In the same way, husbands should love their wives as they do their own bodies. He who loves his wife loves himself. For no one ever hates his own body but he nourishes it and tenderly cares for it, just as Christ does for the church, because we are members of his body" (5:29). Then we have the words of Genesis concerning the "one flesh" of the united man and woman.

In both texts the theme of the Body of Christ is closely linked to the theme of the nuptial union of man and woman as a sign of Christ's relation to the Church (Ephesians 5) and even to the individual Christian (1 Corinthians 6). So that the "organic" union of the body of the Christian with the body of Jesus is described in terms of nuptial love and unity — a union in which, by the power of the Spirit, the "two become one flesh." What I wish to stress here is how, in the use of the phrase from Genesis 2, this redemptive "mystery" (Ephesians 5: 32) is seen to be rooted in and anticipated by the *created* nuptial mystery. But this can only be true because there, "in the beginning," the "two become one flesh," not through the loss of their mutually distinct identities, but in their fruitful complimentarity.

By the mystery of the Incarnation, God has redeemed the creation by establishing such fruitful complimentarity between God and his people in the "one flesh" union of Christ and his church. So it is that history will consummate in the marriage feast of the Lamb and the New Adam. The human destiny is a nuptial destiny. It should go without saying, this divine human complimentarity, is established through the Incarnation by the power of the Spirit, and is not sexual in nature. However, within the created order, a *sign* of this promised union has been established "from the beginning" in what we now call "sexuality."

The sign of marriage shatters, however, if the created complimentary configuration (heterosexuality) of the sign is obscured. Let us explore this claim in relation first to the prohibition of polygamy (and consequently divorce and remarriage) and then to the question of homosexual "unions."

First, the integrity of the sign of sexuality requires the limitation of the "two." *Monogamous* love is inherent in the sign. This Israel had to learn slowly, for Israel had first to live under the gracious pressure of the Lord's "jealously," which we translate into theoretical terms by the concept monotheism. *One God – one spouse*: in the history of revelation, these truths, monotheism and monogamy, are uncovered *as one* at the same moment, in the great prophetic age of Hosea and Ezekiel. So that finally these truths, *one God – one spouse*, were confessed by Israel in that theologically mature and coherent text of Genesis. Placed at the beginning of the canon, this theological "pre-history" served to pass judgment on the polygamy of the patriarchs and kings as a "defection" from the original will of the creator. This is why by the time of Jesus the monogamous ideal was assumed in Israel.[6]

The limit of "two," however, has implications beyond the prohibition of polygamy and adultery. In the Genesis text, "two" is no *mere* numerical designation. It is tied entirely to the two-fold, male-female configuration of the Human Being as made in God's image. Aside from that two-fold configuration, the restriction of marriage to two (as in "a committed relationship between two mature adults") has no coherent rationale. It can only be an arbitrary inhibition, an ethical superstition, or a kind of moral mimicry. As an unreconstructed Mormon might remind us, commitment has, after all, marked many polygamous marriages.

This ought to be obvious enough if human beings may be truly *identified* in sexual terms, not by the inherently two-fold somatic identities as man or woman, but by the several directions the desires of a man or woman might tend, as heterosexual, homosexual, bisexual, etc. The secular gay community has long ago acknowledged such. Following the logic of the current concept of sexual identity by orientation, it understands monogamy to be an oppressive heterosexual value from which "homosexual persons" have been liberated for the natural satisfactions of polyamorous love.[7]

We have used the common jargon by speaking about our "sexuality." It is, however, too small a concept. In speaking about the nuptial nature of the human body, we mean not the capacity for sexual union, as distinct from the totality of somatic existence. We mean rather the capacity for unfettered self-donation — the capacity to find oneself by losing oneself in another. This is the human capacity, by which the Creator generates and nurtures new life. In the beginning, "sexuality" is entirely integrated into the totality of mutual self-giving of marriage. So it was that in their presence one to the other, the man and woman were unashamed in their nakedness (Genesis 2:25). Their bodies could not become "objects" to one another. Their bodies were simply the means of their presence one to another in the self-forgetfulness of unobstructed love.[8]

The nuptial capacity of the body is foundational in creation. It is also, of course, at the genesis of our redemption. This created human capacity for self-donation, redeemed in the self-offering of Jesus' body, becomes by grace the means of our recreation in God's image. "As it was in the beginning, is now, and ever shall be."

The destiny of the body

In 1 Corinthians 6:20 we hear a climactic *ethical* appeal. "Therefore," says Paul, "glorify God in your body." The appeal links this text with chapter 15 in the same epistle, where the theme is the resurrection of the body and the end-time revelation of the glory of God. The sexual ethic of the Christian flows from the body's *baptismal dignity* as member of Christ's body, from its *nuptial nature* given in creation and redeemed by Christ, and from its *promised destiny* through the resurrection of the dead.

Surely the most systematic and sweeping presentation of this promised destiny is in Romans 8. As is typical in the apostle's thought, the relation of the body of the Christian to Christ leads on to the thought of bodily suffering in anticipation of bodily glory (vv. 11, 17). Again also in this text, the early chapters of Genesis are in the background. The whole created order is "waiting for the revealing of the children of God" when the cosmos itself will be "set free from its bondage to decay and will obtain the freedom of the glory of God" (vv. 19, 21). Thus the redemption of the creation (and vindication of the Creator) is tied to the destiny of the human creature as child of God and steward of the creation. The whole content of the great hope can be spoken as "the re-demption of our bodies" (v. 23).

It may also be spoken, in parable and vision, as the great wed-ding, the nuptial consummation, the marriage feast of the Lamb (Rev-elation 22:17). So it is the Christian ethic of the body belongs, not to some discrete "moral concern," but coheres in the first and last things of the bible and in the promises that engulf us in Christ. So it is also that marriage is not simply one among other ethical concerns but is founda-tional, not only to universal human well-being, but to the Christian ethic and ethos; as the nuptial union of the male and female in marriage serves as an "icon" of our human nature and destiny, written into our bodies by our Creator and Redeemer. It is not, as it turns out, theologically incidental that the Bible begins and ends with a marriage.

Consecrated loneliness

Finally, turning back to the concreteness of my pastoral time and place, I ask "What, then, about Monica" (as I will name her here) — that middle-aged woman in the congregation who has never married, who has never "known" a man? What about her and all those who never marry, who are cut off from "sexual fulfillment" by illness, injury, circumstance, or, well, because they have just never found such love? Monica once spoke to her pastor about this, about her loneliness, and about how all the talk in the churches about the importance of "sexual fulfillment" leaves her feeling "out of it." Is the nuptial nature, the iconic dignity, of her body compromised by her singleness, by her never "having sex?" Is her hu-man nature diminished? Does the absence of "sexual experience" leave her somehow less human? Does the true nuptial dignity of her body await the favor a man?

Monica knows the Christian answer to such questions. As she ex-presses it simply: "I do have Jesus, and he was never married." The Word of God Incarnate, the body that hung on the cross and was raised from the dead as the new Human Being, never experienced sexual love. In the dominant ethical pietism ruling in our churches, this fact no longer has theological or ethical significance. But Monica knows what it means. She knows that there are *two* bodily vocations that preserve the nuptial dignity of the body. There is the life of chastity in marriage *or* the life of chastity in singleness. And these two vocations to chastity both point to the same end.

There was a time when the excesses of "holy virginity" needed to be curbed with the recovery of the holiness of the secular vocation of marriage. But how sad, that in this theological recovery, "holy virginity" was in effect simply banished. Monica, and thousands like her, finds no structure of support within the Lutheran churches to consecrate her loneliness to God.

Nevertheless, this is what she has done: consecrate her loneliness to the glory of God, in service to her neighbor and in the church, presenting her body as a living sacrifice in long and intense prayer, in long and intense labor among children and the poor. God has blessed this nuptial offering of her life and made it fruitful. Nor is this thought mere "consolation." By her consecrated singleness she is allowed the freedom to live in bodily fellowship with Jesus, as a living sign of the provisional nature of all created human happiness, even so high and universal happiness as marital love.[9] She is a living anticipation of the coming kingdom, where the redeemed "neither marry nor are given in marriage" (Matthew 22:30) because their nuptial destiny is fulfilled in Christ alone.

She too, with all the baptized, will know the bodily redemption of which marriage is a holy but provisional sign, when our bodies are raised up to be unashamed in the presence of the New Adam, as we are fixed by his gaze and hear his joyful cry: "Here at last is bone of my bone and flesh of my flesh."

Phillip Max Johnson is the pastor of St. Paul Lutheran Church, Jersey City, New Jersey and is the Senior of the Society of the Society of the Holy Trinity, an international fellowship of pastors dedicated to the renewal of the Lutheran pastorate in faith and life.

[1] *Life Together*, trans. J. W. Doberstein (San Francisco: Harper & Row, 1954), 23, 26, 31-39. "Mediated relationship" is my short-hand for the way Bonhoeffer contrasts a humanly constructed "psychic" relationship to the Spirit created "spiritual" relationship. For Bonhoeffer, this is but the extension of the "Biblical and Refon-nation message of the justification of man through grace alone; this alone is the basis of the longing of Christians for one another" (23).

[2] *The Book of Concord*, trans. and ed. T. G. Tappert (Philadelphia: Fortress Press, 1959), 345.

[3] The most profound analysis of the development I know of is in the much neglected work of L. S. Thornton, especially *Revelation and the Modern World*, (Westminster, Great Britain: Dacre Press, 1950). See also the more accessible account, in Gustaf Wingren, *Creation and Law*, trans. R. MacKensie (Philadelphia: Muhlenberg Press, 1961).

[4] Thornton, *Revelation in the Modern World, op. cit.,* pp. 98, 104.

[5] I owe this way of putting it to Wingren, *op. cit.,* p. 37.

[6] For the relation between the joint emergence of monogamy and what is called monotheism in Israel, see Edward Schillebeeckx, *Marriage.- Human Reality and Saving Mystery,* trans. N. D. Smith (London: Sheed and Ward, 1965), 82-94, and John Paul 11, *The Theology of the Body,* (Boston: Pauline Books and Media, 1997), 135-142.

[7] See, for example, D. Y. Rist, "Are Homosexuals Bom That Way?" *The Nation,* October 19, 1992, pp. 424-29.

[8] See John Paul 11, *op. cit.,* pp. 55-57, 70, 111-125 for a highly nuanced meditation on this text and on the coming of "original shame". See also Dietrich Bonhoeffer, *Creation and Fall,* trans. J.C. Fletcher (New York: Macmillan, 1959), 63.

[9] This is but the classical understanding of the holy virginity to be found, for example in the *New Catechism of the Catholic Church,* 1579, 1681, 2233.

Chapter Seven

Homosexuality: A Youth Issue

By Merton P. Strommen

Main-line denominations are being asked to consider a new policy that will sanction the ordination of non-celibate gays and the blessing of same-sex marriages. One wonders why some people within the church have decided to make this theological about-face in policy from a position espoused for centuries and reasserted until recently.

Here are reasons why some may have been influenced to change their minds:

1. Our society's changing view of homosexuality.
2. An unsubstantiated belief that new scientific information has changed the argument.
3. A reinterpretation of Scripture by biblical scholars who favor this change.
4. A response of concern after having heard the painful stories of gays.
5. The linking of opposition to homosexuality with racial discrimination.
6. The influence of a post-Christian society which disparages sexual limits.

Reasons such as these have convinced many in the church that its historic position should be changed and that homosexuality should be equated with heterosexuality. But, for many this proposal is a difficult to evaluate because they have not heard both sides of the argument. They lack a basis for weighing the pros and cons of equating homosexuality with heterosexuality. One reason for this lack is that influential institutions have limited the information they have been giving to only one point of view. Consider how this is true for the following groups.

Prestigious organizations such as the American Psychiatric Association and the much larger American Psychological Association (APA) have established policy statements that equate homosexuality with heterosexuality. As a result their committees and publications have become vehicles for influencing courts, legislatures and public opinion. The political stance of these mental health organizations has made it difficult, virtually impossible, to fund research that contests their position or to publish articles opposing their policy statements. This politicization of homosexuality represents a highly unusual decision because these institutions usually establish policy on the basis of scientific evidence. There is no question but that their actions have introduced a distinct chill factor into the scientific community on the subject of homosexuality.

Psychologists and psychiatrists who have disagreed with their organization's decision realized that a separate group was needed to continue the scientific study of prevention, treatment, and problems associated with homosexuality. So they formed a group in 1992 known as the National Association for Research and Therapy of Homosexuality. This group of about 1500 psychiatrists, psychologists, and mental health workers, though committed to the scientific process, has nevertheless been actively opposed by the American Psychological Association.

The APA president, Dr. Linda Johnson wrote an editorial, for instance, in which she called for scientific freedom in research, debate, and academia, regardless of the level of controversy involved. She wrote, "I am strongly supportive of open debate in the APA regardless of the intensity or volume of the debate. Debate is healthy. Disagreement is healthy." No doubt she had in mind the strong criticisms ("a political storm") that the APA received from Congress for an article in one of its official journals commending pedophilia as being, in many cases, normal and healthy.

Acting on her comments, two members of the APA, psychiatrist A. Dean Byrd and psychologist Joseph Nicolosi wrote her to commend her interest in scientific freedom. They requested that therapists be permitted to make a case in APA publications for therapy aimed at modifying unwanted homosexuality. They also requested that meetings of the National Association of Research and Therapy for Homosexuals be announced in the official publication of APA, the *Monitor*, a right now freely granted gay and lesbian groups. Instead of answering their letter, Linda Johnson referred it to Clinton Anderson, Officer of Gay, Lesbian, and Bisexual Concerns. He wrote the two psychiatrists, indicating that "reorientation therapy" should be excluded from the scientific debate. (NARTH, 2001)

A further example is found in the words of psychologist Robert Perloff, the 1985 president of the American Psychological Association, who expressed open anger and frustration in his speech at the APA Annual Convention in 2001. He condemned the APA's one-sided political activism with respect to its policy against reorientation therapy of homosexuals. He said: "You consider such therapy unethical.... That's all wrong. First, the data are not fully in yet. Second, if the client wants a change, listen to the client. Third, you're barring research. How can you do research on change if therapists involved in this work are threatened with being branded as unethical?" (*Monitor* 2001)

Freedom of thought and expression of alternative views on homosexuality is not a characteristic of faculty in today's colleges and Universities. An example is found in the Code of Ethics for Social workers established at St. Cloud University Minnesota. "It is simply not acceptable for social workers to view homosexual people as sinners.... The only legitimate position...is to abhor the oppression...and to act professionally and personally to end the degradation (of homosexuals)." It is suggested that a Catholic student or any student who can not agree should leave the degree program. (Lerner, 1993) This Code of Ethics is found in many other universities as well.

Another illustration is found in the actions of the Stanford University Law and Policy Review Board. It asked that articles be solicited that focused on whether homosexuality is associated with medical or psychological harm. It chose authors who would represent both traditional and pro-gay points of view. When the Stanford Policy Review editors and staff read the shocking evidence of medical and psychological harm created by homosexuality, however, they reversed their decision. They chose to publish only the pro-gay articles. (The ones they refused to publish are now available through the Regent University Law Review (www.regent/acad/schlaw/law review/)). (Clevenger, 2001-2)

Marketing homosexuality
Little is known about the dark side of homosexuality. It relates to a successful effort to use the media to normalize homosexuality in the public's eye and avoid articles that report negative aspects of homosexuality. Persons who publicly expose the dark side are quickly discredited. This media stance is the result of a deliberate effort of gay

activists to market the concept of homosexuality to America. Two Harvard graduates, Marshall Kirk and Hunter Madsen authored a "conspiracy marketing plan" in 1989. The purpose of their plan is to "normalize" homosexuality in the public eye. To accomplish their purpose they identified two strategies: "First you get your foot in the door by being as similar as possible.... If you use idealistic gay advertisements it makes no difference that the ads are lies, not to us, because you're using them to ethically good effect."

The second strategy is this: "The public should be persuaded that gays are victims of circumstances, that they no more choose their orientation than their height. For all practical purposes, gays should be considered to have been born gay." (Kirk & Madsen, 1989)

The marketing document (which has been followed with great success) ends with a call to discredit, intimidate, and silence opponents. Instead of allowing free and open debate, the authors advocate desensitizing mainstream America to bi/homosexuality by "jamming" any contrary information and mobilizing sympathetic political forces.

Legal threats are being mounted against organizations accused of "discrimination" against homosexuals. The Boy Scouts is one such organization, accused of being discriminatory because they decided not to allow openly active gays to serve as Scout leaders. Their decision, contested in courts of law all the way to the Supreme Court, has made it difficult for the Scouts. Many public schools and funding agencies — who assume the leaders are guilty of discrimination — have cut off funds they traditionally gave the Scouts. Few of these donors, however, know the reason why the Scouts took their much contested stand.

Here is the story: a California family sued the Scouts in 1993 for exposing their son to a Scout leader who molested him. In the subsequent suit, the Scouts were ordered to turn over 25,000 pages of documents to the plaintiff. This unprecedented disclosure revealed that thousands of boys had been molested by Scout leaders and other volunteers between the years 1971 and 1991, resulting in the expulsion of over 1,800 Scout volunteers for ephebophile (or post-pubescent) activity. The documents showed that some Scout leaders molested over 40 such boys before getting caught. (Amici Curiae, 1999, Geissinger, 1993)

Yet the North American Man-Boy Love Association chose to write a letter of protest to the national Scout office "urging the Boy Scouts of America to cease its discrimination against openly gay or lesbian persons in the appointment of its scout masters and scouters in its membership." (Stevenson, 1992)

Another illustration of intimidation through legal action is found in the action of the legislators in Sweden's parliament in May 2002. They passed the first reading of a bill criminalizing "hate speech" against homosexuals. While the bill targets Nazi and racist hate campaigns, it also includes church sermons! Prominent homosexuals have said publicly that they will report Church of Sweden pastors who "speak disparagingly" about homosexual behavior from the pulpit. (World Report, 2002)

I find it significant that heterosexism – the value system that prizes heterosexuality and devalues homosexuality – is viewed by gay activists as an evil equal to racism and a point of view that should be eliminated. Just as persons accused of racism face employment discrimination and are deemed unfit for public office, the equivalent sanctions can be leveled at heterosexists. Some gay activists demand that heterosexism be eliminated from all institutions including religious institutions. If a patient wishes to change from a homosexual to a heterosexual orientation for religious reasons, some therapists encourage a "religious reorientation." (Schreier, 1988)

Many public schools are both adopting curricula to present homosexuality as normal and are encouraging homosexual clubs for students.

The position of some public schools presents another deterrent to a free and open discussion. The book, *Heather Has Two Mommies,* published by Alyson Publications, is currently being used in many public school systems. Besides introducing courses on homosexuality into the life of the school, school administrators are inviting gay activists to serve as "adult advisors" to youth confused about their sexuality, or who think they are gay. (Herdt, 1989)

The Division of Outreach Ministry of the Evangelical Lutheran Church in America is promoting a pro-gay point of view. In May of 1996 the division's board of directors voted: "To encourage the staff of the Division for Outreach to engage in dialogue with our lesbian sisters and gay brothers to discuss and explore outreach options to the lesbian and gay communities. The staff will dialogue with groups such as leaders of Lutherans Concerned" (an independent organization designed to promote the gay point of view).

An outcome of the division's "Gay and Lesbian Hospitality Study" (carried out by a committee representing several divisions and commissions of the Church), was a three-ringed binder notebook entitled, "Congregational Hospitality to Gay and Lesbian People." Published in 1999, the notebook provides information for congregations to become

"Reconciling in Christ" congregations. The printed text makes it clear that becoming a welcoming congregation "is not the end product" but rather a "journey or process that could result in conversations about other gay and lesbian issues in the church, such as performing blessing ceremonies and the question of the ordination of gay and lesbian people." The notebook's bibliography, some 28 references, reflects a pro-gay stance. Two of these books teach that the Bible is not against homosexuality. (Division for Outreach, 1999)

These six influential groups have limited their information to one side of the issue. This makes it difficult for people lacking information that contests their position, to evaluate the reasons now being given for a proposed change. They need to know the implications that are present in making such a revolutionary change. Following are some which I see as a psychologist and as a youth researcher.

What research has established

There is widespread misunderstanding with respect to the findings of scientific research. People are insisting that scientific research has established these three assumptions: (a) One is born a homosexual; (b) it cannot be altered; and (c) it is normal and healthy. What many do not realize is that these three assumptions have **not** been established as fact. They are not true. They are no more than unproven hypotheses.

Some will insist that studies exist which "prove" that a man is born homosexual and has no choice in the matter. The studies they might identify are those of Simon LeVay, Dean H. Hammer, and J.M. Bailey. Though other studies might be mentioned, these are the authors primarily responsible for the popular and politicized impression that being homosexual is something that cannot be helped. It is significant that all three men have acknowledged in later writings that their studies do **not** establish what they had hoped to "prove."

Bailey, co-author of the most influential twin study on homosexuality, repeated his study, using a large random sample (4,900) drawn from a registry of twins in Australia. Instead of finding the concordance rates for identical male twins to be 100 percent (the expected percentage if homosexuality is genetic), the rates were 11 percent (Jones & Yarhouse, 2000)

Friedman and Downey in their book, Sexual Orientation and Psychoanalysis: Sexual Science and Clinical Practice, answer the question: "Is homosexuality genetic?" They write: "At clinical conferences one often hears discussants commenting that 'homosexuality is genetic' and, therefore, that homosexual orientation is fixed and unmodifiable. Neither assertion is true." (Friedman &Downey, 2002)

A survey in 1993 by the American Psychiatric Association 's Office on International Affairs, established the fact that a majority of psychiatrists, internationally view homosexuality as a developmental disorder. They see it as a disorder that lacks the capacity to deliver the health and the wholeness usually found in heterosexuality.

But most gays are convinced they were born gay. What do we know about the early development of homosexuality? Here is what we know at this time.

What we know

There is a genetic predisposition known to exist for homosexuals. The disposition is seen in such characteristics as a greater than average sensitivity, shyness, intelligence, and esthetic interest—characteristics often associated with effeminacy. Such predisposing characteristics do not however determine that one will become homosexual. They only increase a person's vulnerability to subsequent familial, psychological, social, and environmental factors.

To illustrate, my five sons have a predisposition to athletics. If their blood corpuscles were examined they would be found in the shape of a football, baseball or basketball. But their predisposition to athletics did not determine they would become basketball players. That was largely determined by their dad's interest in the game, the emphasis given basketball at their schools, and the enjoyment of the sport by friends who surrounded our home. Whitehead, a scientist who studied the influence of a genetic disposition, estimates that it has a 10 percent influence on a person becoming homosexual (Whitehead, 1999).

What accounts for the other 90 percent? A number of factors can be identified. One centers in prenatal sex steroid hormones and the influence of prenatal androgen. It is hypothesized that a deficit results in male homosexuality and a surplus of androgen results in female homosexuality (Friedman & Downey, 2002).

Another factor is the internal psychological environment of a child. Identical twins can remember their father's actual behavior in similar fashion but value it differently. They will describe the same father as detached and withdrawn. Yet another factor—and a very important one—is a child's relationship to mother and father. In infancy, both boys and girls are emotionally attached to the mother. The mother is the first love object. Girls can continue to develop their feminine identification with their mother. But the boy has an additional developmental task. He must "dis-identify" from mother and identify with father.

Between the ages of two and four a boy needs to discover his masculinity. The father helps him do this by playing with him, helping him to become conscious of his maleness. If father is too busy with his work, or loves his golf too much this help will be missing. If the boy is especially sensitive, he will be inclined to cling to his mother and not identify with his absent father. Over time the boy's gender can become distorted.

Extreme evidences of this distortion are found in children who have a Gender Identity Disorder, known as GID. This is seen in boys who shun rough and tumble games and chooses girl activities. Or, it is seen in girls who prefer to dress and act as a boy. If this distortion is not treated, 75 percent will end up as adult homosexuals. But the condition is treatable. A father and mother can end the distortion if they are shown what they need to do. (Nicolosi, 2002)

Environmental factors

There are other environmental factors that can contribute to development of same-sex attraction. These include such factors as sexual activity with other boys, sexual abuse by an adult, exposure to pornographic literature, and personal decisions. Clearly, homosexuality is a developmental disorder that can be modified and even corrected. One is not born a homosexual nor is it a fixed condition.

Intolerance shown advocates of reorientation

There is a wide spread resistance to "reorientation therapy." One obvious reason for the resistance is this. If it can be demonstrated that some people do change their orientation, it puts a lie to the idea that everyone is born a homosexual and the orientation cannot be altered.

Many responsible people are claiming there is no scientific evidence that reparative therapy is effective. Because this claim is being given wide publicity it bears further scrutiny. We can begin by noting how studies are carried out by scientists. Professor Stephen Hawking, the renowned theoretical physicist, gives the following account of how scientific inquiry is conducted:

> A good theory will describe a large range of phenomena on the basis of a few simple postulates and will make definite predictions that can be tested. If the predictions agree with the observations, the theory survives that test, though it can

never be proved to be correct. On the other hand, if the observations disagree with the predictions, one has to discard or modify the theory.

At least that is what is supposed to happen. In practice, people often question the accuracy of the observations and the reliability and moral character of those making the observations. (Hawking, 2001)

Note that scientific inquiry proceeds by presenting a theoretical statement or hypothesis which then can be tested. Evidence is summoned that will support either the acceptance or rejection of the hypothesis. Note also, that evidence which supports the hypothesis does not prove that it is correct. It only strengthens the likelihood that what is proposed squares with reality. That is why a number of confirmatory studies are needed.

What a scientist needs

A scientist begins with a hypothesis such as: "Change from homosexual to heterosexual orientation is possible for some." Such a hypothesis is a necessary first step before marshalling evidence that either supports or rejects it. The evidence that is used needs to be secured through scientific procedures using such means as a survey, controlled interviews, or methodologically precise experiments with control groups.

Granted, the evidence gained in the social sciences varies considerably in reliability. Hence, grading the strength (or reliability) of the evidence is commonly done. In the medical sciences this is done by the Institute for Clinical Systems Improvement. Their people evaluate the strength of the evidence on the basis of the study design, sample size, and patient population. The study is assigned one of four grades: Grade I — supported by good evidence; Grade II — supported by fair evidence; Grade III — supported by limited evidence; and Grade IV — supported only by opinion. (Greer, Mosser, Logan & Halaas, 2000)

It is important to note that most studies reporting a degree of success with "conversion therapy" appeared in professional journals during the 1950s, 1960s and 1970s. But following the big "chill" in research that occurred after the decision of the American Psychiatric Association in 1973, the number of studies diminished rapidly (due to a lack of funding and the reluctance of editors to publish articles contesting the position of the American Psychiatric Association).

Warren Throckmorton has analyzed and reported on 83 studies on the therapeutic process of conversion therapy. While some are lacking in sophisticated methodology (and hence may be accorded a Grade II or Grade III ranking), they nevertheless support the hypothesis that conversion therapy is effective for some people. (Throckmorton, 1998)

Following his review, Throckmorton authored another article — one that required two years for peer review — that was published in an official journal of the American Psychological Association in June of 2002. The article is unique in that it presents eleven studies of "ex-gays" which identify a religious faith as contributing to the process of changing from homosexual attractions to heterosexual ones. (Throckmorton, 2002).

Throckmorton's article begins with a quote from F. Worthen: "What does 'ex-gay' mean? It is a statement of fact. I am no longer the same. God has changed me, He is changing me, and He most certainly will continue to change me."

Worthen continues: "At New Hope Ministry, we do not attempt to make heterosexuals out of homosexuals. Rather, we attempt to change a person's identity, the way a person looks at himself. We encourage the former gay to drop the label homosexual from his life. However, we do not ask him to become dishonest about his struggle with homosexuality. He is a Christian who has a homosexual problem, rather than a homosexual who believes in Jesus Christ."

Testing the hypothetical

Now back to the business of testing a hypothesis. When Spitzer, chair of the committee that removed homosexuality from the category of mental illness, became interested in the reversibility of homosexuality, he began interviewing persons who had been ex-gays five years or more. He reported his findings at the May 2001 convention of the American Psychiatric Association.

His first slide made it apparent that the hypothesis he had been holding was this — "Homosexual behavior...can never be changed." The slide read: "There is a professional consensus that homosexual behavior can be resisted, renounced or relabeled but that homosexual orientation can never be changed." His next slide read: "I certainly shared this viewpoint."

He then described how he had talked with some ex-gays who had been picketing the 1999 APA meeting. They claimed that contrary to a recent APA position statement, change of sexual orientation was possible. After much thought he decided to study the self-reported experiences of individuals who claim to have achieved a change from homosexual to heterosexual attraction.

The evidence resulting from his interviews of 200 (143 males and 57 females) by telephone caused him to reject the hypothesis he had been holding. He indicated this in the slide that read: "Contrary to conventional wisdom, some highly motivated individuals, using a variety of change efforts, can make substantial change in multiple indicators of sexual orientation and achieve good heterosexual functioning. Subjects that made less substantial changes still believed that such changes were extremely beneficial."

Here is what he reported as evidence. During the year prior to initiating change 99 percent of the male sample and 88 percent of the females affirmed that they had same-sex sexual fantasies, while after they had experienced change only 32 percent of the men and five percent of the women reported the same type of fantasies. A desire for emotional involvement with same-sex individuals went from 78 percent of the men and 81 percent of the women to eight percent of men and four percent of women post-change. (Spitzer, manuscript under review) Though one can identify methodological limitations in Spitzer's study, the evidence is compelling.

Similar results are found in the questionnaire study by Nicolosi, Byrd, and Potts involving 882 ex-gays. These respondents had sought help because they were dissatisfied with their orientation. The survey showed that approximately seven years after initiating a change, 34 percent could report that much change towards heterosexuality had occurred, and 43 percent could report some change. This evidence gives strong support to the hypothesis that reorientation is possible for some.(Nicolosi, Byrd, & Potts, 2001).

Increasing numbers of youth becoming homosexuals

In my book, *The Church and Homosexuality: Searching for a Middle Ground*, I note the confusion of adolescent males regarding their sexual orientation. It is a time when they are especially vulnerable to the influence of their social environment. They do not know how to distinguish between same-sex attractions — common to this age group — and the serious implications of giving themselves to homosexual practices.

Clinicians have noticed a growing number of thirteen, fourteen, and fifteen year old boys announcing to their parents that they are gay. This transition which used to occur in the mid to late twenties is now taking place in the early and mid teens.

If major church bodies decide to ordain committed homosexuals and bless same-sex marriages, it will be seen as equating homosexuality with heterosexuality. It will be interpreted in the minds of people as a decision of the church that homosexuality is an orientation also created by God with no inherent dangers. It will be assumed that the orientation should henceforth be viewed as normal and lauded as good. Should the moral guardians of our nation take such a position, school administrators will be encouraged to adopt a program of homosexual advocacy groups.

Sexual diversity is actively being promoted in many schools; some are mandated by state law. Some of these advocacy programs openly encourage homosexuality as an orientation youth should consider. Some advocacy programs reflect a world view that stands in opposition to a biblical position, including: the redefinition of marriage and family; a refusal to recognize the central importance of both mothers and fathers in child development; support for the children's autonomy from authority; a "sex-positive" approach that sees all forms of sexual expression as valid.

A quotation from a ninth grade text book in one of the Boston schools illustrates this world view. It reads: "Testing your ability to function sexually and give pleasure to another person maybe less threatening in the early teens with people of your own sex." The textbook also advises children that they may, in fact "come to the conclusion that growing up means rejecting the values of your parents." (Rondeau, 2002)

The dark side of homosexuality

When considering the issue of a gay lover we need to recognize that the homosexual community includes two very different groups of people. One is the highly visible group we see in church and communities including those who tell their stories in church. The other is the group whose private face we seldom see.

The first group consists of devout gays and lesbians who are active in our congregations, people living in committed relationships, and contributing to the welfare of our country. They include pastors, theologians, professional people, and devoted citizens. Many are children of church members, children of pastors, children of people we know and respect. Without question most of these people in their hearts have reconciled their orientation with Scripture and have found a way of coping with their same-sex attractions.

The second and possibly larger group of homosexuals presents a far different face. What they do and say is generally kept private and away from public scrutiny. It is an aspect of homosexuality seldom made public because it involves the dark side of homosexuality. One need not consider the darkest side — the "bath house" gay culture, or the gay "parks," or the gay bars which are involved in the promiscuous, gay-on-the-prowl-for-sex aspect of homosexuality. That side of homosexuality is graphically told by Frank Browning, a journalist, in his book *The Culture of Desire*. It is enough for this essay to single out one aspect which immediately affects youth.

It relates to the desire of many adult gays for an adolescent boy as lover. It is a characteristic found in far greater incidence among homosexuals than in heterosexual men's desire for adolescent girls. According to the authoritative *Encyclopedia of Homosexuality* this sexual desire of homosexual males for a teenage boy is to be expected. It says: "Until very recently man/boy love relationships were accepted as a part, and indeed, a major part of male homosexuality." (Dynnes, 1990)

The first homosexual encounter reported in the study by 882 ex-gays, occurred at the average age of 11. The average age of the persons initiating the encounter was 17. (Nicolosi, Byrd, & Potts, 2001). This illustrates how boys are usually introduced to homosexual practices by an older person. Such is the pattern being discovered through the scandal now rocking the Catholic Church. The Official Catholic Directory of Catholic University reports that of the 539 reporting sexual abuse by a priest, 91 percent were males. Of the 189 victims whose age at the time of the abuse is known, 80 percent were between the ages of 10 and 18. (DeBarros, 2002)

In the early days of Rome, Sparta, and Athens it was common for homosexual men to have an adolescent boy as lover. When the boy became an adult, he continued the cycle by finding a boy to love sexually. As a result of this practice, the historian, Boswell estimates that one half to a majority of men in these cities were involved in homosexual practices. (Boswell, 1980)

Today there is a North American Man-Boy Love Association (LAMBLA) that openly promotes sex with minor boys. It claims that boy-lovers respond to the needs of boys they love.

Indicative of this point of view is a book published by The University of Minnesota Press entitled, *Harmful to Minors: The Perils of Protecting Children from Sex*. The author, Judith Levine, contends that there is no proof that "it's always harmful for kids to have sexual relationships with adults.... A boy's experience with a priest could be reported as positive." (O'Keefe, 2002)

With such a stance characterizing many in the homosexuality movement it is not surprising that prostitution involving boys should become open and evident. In 1995, Judith Reisman of the Institute for Media Education made a content analysis of advertisements in the nation's most influential homosexual newspaper, *The Advocate*. She found that 63 percent of the personal ads sought or offered prostitution. Many of them openly solicited boys. (Reisman & Johnson, 1995)

In her article, "Crafting Bi/Homosexual Youth," Reisman also reports that some homosexual leaders are determined to gain access to schools, scouts, and other child institutions in order to "institutionalize socialization techniques to bring homosexuality to mainstream youth." (Reisman, 2002) Inasmuch as one fourth of adolescent males are confused over their sexual orientation, they are especially vulnerable to such recruiting efforts.

A threatening aspect of adult males recruiting young people as lovers is reflected in two major studies conducted by Shrier & Johnson.. They conclude that sexually abused youth are up to seven times more likely to become adult homosexuals than comparable youth not abused. (Shrier & Johnson, 1985, 1988) This suggests that if the predatory quality of such males is allowed free course, one can expect to see an increase in the population of homosexuals beyond the three percent where it is now.

Health risks for youth

A teenager who self-identifies as gay is at high risk from three threatening illnesses: 1) for infection with HIV or another sexually transmitted disease; 2) for psychiatric problems including suicidal ideation; and, 3) for self-destructive behaviors such as drug and alcohol abuse and prostitution. (Nicolosi, 2002). A recent study by Garofalo has documented the life style factors that are associated with homosexual adolescents. At least twice as many such adolescents are likely to have engaged in one of 30 high health risk behaviors (Garofalo, 2002)

Consider the seriousness of AIDS. During the past 20 years, more Americans have died from AIDS (442,853) than died in combat in World War I and World War II. Half of these deaths are due to promiscuous homosexual activity. (Sepkowitz, 2001)

Consider adolescent boys ages 13-24. The Center of Disease Control reported that as of the year 2000 over 15,000 teenagers were infected with the disease as a result of sex with adult men. (Center for Disease Control, 2002) Another study, "AIDS among Adolescents," in

1990 reported that at least 59 percent of adolescents with AIDS were directly infected by adult homosexuals. (Brownworth, 1992) Victoria Brownworth when reporting this information used this as the title for her article, "America's Worst Kept Secret: Aids is Devastating the Nation's Teenagers and Our Kids are Dying by the Thousands."

This is an epidemic that no one seems to want to talk about.

To hide the fact that most AIDS children appear to be infected by bi/homosexuals, the "World AIDS Day" brochure artfully reported that 16 percent of adolescents, aged 13 through 19, have been infected through heterosexual contact," rather than to report that 84 percent of AIDS children were infected by male homosexual abuse (Tennessee State Department of Education, 1995).

Protection by the media

It is evident that little information has been made public regarding this dark and ominous side of homosexuality. Providing it now is neither homophobic nor discriminatory. On the contrary, to withhold such information would be unethical. The implications for adolescent males are serious. Should the nation's moral guardians identify homosexuality as something God blesses and honors as good?

People of faith do well to conclude that the Holy Scripture inspired by God, present the proper guide for living. The sexual boundaries which it identifies have been established in the best interests of not only individuals but also families and society. The unique wisdom reflected in God's Holy Writ goes beyond human understanding.

Merton P. Strommen is a pastor, a research psychologist, and founder of the Search Institute and the Youth and Family Institute. He is author of The Church & Homosexuality: Searching for a Middle Ground *(Kirk House Publishers; 2001).*

References

American Psychiatric Association, "Psychiatrists' Views of Homosexuality," *Psychiatric News*. September 1993, a survey conducted by the APA's Office of International Affairs
Amici Curiae.Brief, 1999, Public Advocate et al. Dale vs. Boy Scouts of America, 734 A 2d, 1196 (N.J.) (No.99-699)

Bailey, Michael, Michael Dunne & Nicolas G. Martin, "Genetic and Environmental Influences on Sexual Orientation and Its Correlates in an Australian Twin Sample" *Journal of Personality and Social Psychology*, 78, March2000, 33

Boswell ,John, 1980, *Christianity, Social Tolerance and Homosexuality*, University of Chicago Press, Chicago, 54-55.

Brownworth, Victoria A., "America's Worst Kept Secret: AIDS is Devastating the Nation's Teenagers and Our Kids are Dying by the Thousands" *The Advocate*, 40-41, March 24, 1992.

Clevenger, Ty, 2001-2002, "Gay Orthodoxy and Academic Heresy," Regent University Law Review, Vol.14, No.2, p. 241.

Center for Disease Control and Prevention. "Young People at Risk: HIV Among American Youth." March 2002

DeBarros, Anthony, "The Accusers and the Accused", *US Today*, The Official Catholic Directory, The Catholic University, November 11, 2002, 7D

Dynnes, Wayne ed. 1990 *Encyclopedia of Homosexuality*, Garland Publications, Kentucky, Taylor Francis Distributors, 964

Friedman, Richard & Jennifer I. Downey, 2002, *Sexual Orientation and Psychoanalysis: Sexual Science and Clinical Practice*. Columbia University Press: New York.

Garofalo,R.,R. Wolf, S. Kessel, J. Palfrey, R. Durant,1998, "The association between health risk behaviors and sexual orientation among a school-based sample of adolescents (Youth Risk Behavior Survey) *Pediatrics*, Vol., 101, No. 5, p. 895-903.

Geissinger, Steve, "Scouts Remove 1800 Scoutmasters for Suspected Abuse Over Two Decades" Associated Press, October 14, 1993

Greer, N. , G. Mosser, G. Logan, G. Halaas, 2000, "A practical approach to evidence grading," *Joint Commission Journal on Quality Improvement*, Vol. 26, 700-712.

Hawking, Stephen, *The Universe in a Nutshell*, NY: Bantam Books, 2001.

Hendin, Herbert, 1996, *Suicide in America*, W.W. Norton & Co.: New York.

Herdt. Gilbert, 1989, "Introduction: Gay and Lesbian Youth, Emergent Identities and Cultural Scenes at Home and Abroad." In *Gay Lesbian Youth*, page 4.

Jones, Stanton L. & Mark A. Yarhouse, 2000. *Homosexuality: The Use of Scientific Research in the Church's Moral Debate*, Downers Grove: InterVarsity Press, 77

Kirk, Marshall & Hunter Madsen, 1989, After the Ball: How America Will Conquer its Fear and Hatred of Gays in the 90's, "Portfolio of Pro-Gay Advertising," pp.146, 178, 216-45.

Lerner, Maura. "St. Cloud State Department Statement on Gay Causes Backlash." *Star Tribune*, Minneapolis, June 1993

Monitor on Psychology, Publication of the American Psychological Association, December 2001, page 20.

NARTH Bulletin, "Can NARTH Be Denied the Right to Advertise in APA Publications?" Vol.10, No.3, December 2001, 16-17.

Newman, Lawrence E., 1996, "Treatment for the Parents of Effeminate Boys" *American Journal of Psychiatry*, Vol.133, No. 5, 687

Nicolosi, Joseph & Linda Ames, 2002, *A Parents Guide to Preventing Homosexuality*, Intervarsity Press: Downers Grove, Ill. pages 44-45

Nicolosi, Joseph, A. Dean Byrd, & W. Potts, "Retrospective Changes in Sexual Orientation: A Consumer Survey of Conversion Clients" Psychological Reports, June 2002.

O'Keefe, Mark. "Some in mainstream contend certain cases of adult-minor sex should be acceptable." *Star Tribune*, March 26, 2002.

Reisman, Judith & Charles B. Johnson,1995, "Partner Solicitation Language As a Reflection of Male Sexual Orientation." *The Briefing Book*, 169.

Reisman, Judith, 2001-2002, "Crafting Bi/Homosexual Youth" *Regent University Law Review* Vol. 14, No.2, 322

Remafedi, G., J. Farrow, R. Deisher, "Risk Factors for Attempted Suicide in Gay and Bisexual Youth," *Pediatrics*, Vol.87, No. 6, June 1991, 869-875.

Rondeau, Paul E., 2001-2202, "Selling Homosexuality to America," Regent University Law Review, 479.

Schreier, Barry, 1988, "Of Shoes and Ships and Sealing Wax: The Faulty and Specious Assumptions of Sexual Reorientation Therapies," Vol. 20, *Mental Health Counseling*, p. 305, 308.

Sepkowitz,Kent A., "AIDSCThe First 20Years," *New England Journal of Medicine*, Vol.344, No.23, 1764, June 2001.

Shier, Diane & Robert L. Johnson, 1985, "Sexual Victimization of Boys: Experience at an Adolescent Medicine Clinic," 6, *Journal of Adolescent Health* Car, 372.

Shrier, Diane & Robert L. Johnson, 1988, "Sexual Victimization of Boys: An Ongoing Study of an Adolescent Medicine Clinic Population," 80 J Nat. Med Assoc. 1189.

Stevenson, Leland. Letter from Co-Recording Secretary, NAMBLA, to Ben Love, Boy Scout Executive, November 1992

Tennessee State Department of Education, 1995, Lifetime Wellness Curriculum Framework, Lifetime Wellness Resource Manual, (1994-95) (recommending the "The World AIDS Day" brochure in Section IV as "Resources" to be taught to Tennessee teachers as a sex education curricula from August 1994 to March 1995.

Throckmorton, Warren, 1998, "Attempts to Modify Sexual Orientation: A Review of Outcome Literature and Ethical Issues." *The Journal of Mental Health Counseling*, Vol.20, 283-304.

Throckmorton, Warren, "Empirical Findings Concerning Ex-Gays: Initial Findings Concerning the Change Process, *Journal of Professional Psychology: Research and Practice*, June 2002.

Whitehead, Neil & Briar Whitehead, 1999, *My Genes Made Me Do It: A Scientific Look at Sexual Reorientation.* Huntington House Publishers, 107- 108

World Report, "Hate Speech' law could chill sermons," *Christianity Today*, August 5, 2002, page 22.

�֎ Chapter Eight

Does the Bible Regard Same-Sex Intercourse as Intrinsically Sinful?

By Robert A. J. Gagnon

Does one have to disregard the clear witness in Scripture in order to approve of some homosexual practice? Or can one heed Scripture's anti-homosex, pro-complementarity witness even as one finds ways to accommodate some homosexual unions? In short, can Scripture's normative opposition to homosexual practice be combined with a policy of "exceptions"?

This is an important question for persons who regard the Bible as the church's supreme authority in matters of faith and practice and yet wonder whether the church should make some provision for homosexual relationships. The answer to this question hinges on at least three other considerations:

(1)   Does the Bible depict homosexual practice as intrinsically sinful or as normally sinful?

(2)   In particular, do the creation stories in Genesis 1-2 preclude, as a matter of course, all same-sex intercourse? Or can they be faithfully interpreted as witnesses for committed homosexual unions?

(3)   Do we have significantly new knowledge today about "homosexual orientation" to warrant an adjustment — though not rejection — of Scripture's stance against homosexual practice?

The purpose of this essay is to address these crucial questions.

Why this essay? To be sure, I have dealt with these three questions in other work, most notably in *The Bible and Homosexual Practice:*

Texts and Hermeneutics (Abingdon, 2001) and in my more recent and shorter synthesis, *Homosexuality and the Bible: Two Views* (Fortress, 2003). So why write this article? There are two answers to that question.

One answer is simply that more needs to be said about each of these three questions. Question (1) is important enough to merit a more focused treatment. As regards questions (2) and (3) I have done more extensive work since the publication of *The Bible and Homosexual Practice*. Owing to space constraints, these materials could not be adequately incorporated into *Homosexuality and the Bible*. Readers will get from this article the most extensive critique to date of the "orientation argument" (question 3) so often employed by prohomosex apologists. They will also get from this author a much fuller presentation of the relevance of the creation texts to the homosexuality issue.

The second reason for this essay is that a new article has come out that makes the case for exceptions. The article, "The Bible and Homosexuality," is by Mark Allan Powell, professor of New Testament at Trinity Lutheran Seminary, a well-published scholar who takes Scripture seriously. His essay appears in a book that "was initiated by the ELCA seminary presidents in response to a churchwide mandate" to study the feasibility of blessing homosexual unions: *Faithful Conversations: Christian Perspectives on Homosexuality* (ed. James M. Childs, Jr.; Fortress Press, 2003; pp. 19-40 = Powell's article). Other scholars, such as Martti Nissinen and Bernadette Brooten, have made more detailed and sweeping cases for approval of homosexual behavior. But Powell's article will probably be more influential, certainly within the Evangelical Lutheran Church in America, for three reasons. (1) It appears as the only essay written by a biblical scholar in a book being promoted as a study guide for ELCA churches. (2) It is a concise, well organized, and easy read. (3) In acknowledging that the biblical prohibitions of homosexual practice cannot be dismissed, Powell's article makes enough criticisms of prohomosex readings of Scripture to come across to some as a moderate or centrist reading. As I will show, this would be a mistaken perception, but it is a perception that nonetheless has to be reckoned with. In sum, unlike some other prohomosex treatments, Powell's has a strong chance of appealing to the middle of the church, with disastrous consequences.

Because Powell makes the best argument for "exceptions" to a normative policy of opposition to same-sex intercourse, I will use his article as my main conversation partner for addressing the three questions raised above.[1] It is not necessary for readers of this article to read Powell's essay in order to understand *my* argument. This is not to say that I am using Powell's article as a mere foil for my own points, or that I am unconcerned about how accurately I represent his positions. On the contrary, readers of my online[2] material will see from section I a very close reading of Powell's article. Rather, I am asserting that the positions to which I am responding are laid out with enough detail to enable the reader to follow the discussion without Powell's essay in hand. Obviously, if readers want to evaluate for themselves whether I have correctly understood Powell's argument, they will need to read both Powell's essay and my online[3]material. But the three main sections of my essay can be evaluated in their own right.[4]

Although this essay interacts with the work of a Lutheran scholar (Powell) and is part of this volume addressing the current discussion in the ELCA concerning homosexuality, the concerns raised in this essay transcend distinctively Lutheran issues. In dialoguing on the homosexuality issue in different mainline Christian denominations, it never ceases to amaze me how often prohomosex apologists cite their specific denominational heritage as allowing them to circumvent Scripture's strong witness to a heterosexual prerequisite. The claim usually begins with a line like: "Unlike persons from other denominations, we [fill in the blank: Lutherans, Episcopalians, Presbyterians, Methodists, Mennonites, etc.] interpret Scripture in such-and-such a way." The fact is, there are no interpretive methods or theological concerns, distinctive to any mainline Christian denomination, which lead to a prohomosex position. There is nothing distinctively Lutheran about Powell's presentation; nor, for that matter, is there anything distinctively Presbyterian about mine. This is not a sectarian debate.

I. Does Powell advocate exceptions?

The full online[4] section provides a detailed analysis of Powell's presentation, showing that Powell is insistent about three key points that invariably lead to the personal aside expressed at the end of his article.

1. While the Bible depicts homosexual practice as "normally contrary to God's will" and "intrinsically unnatural," it does not view such behavior as "intrinsically sinful." By "not intrinsically sinful" Powell means that *approval* of some homosexual activity is possible, at least hypothetically (pp. 21-22, 26, 28, 35).

2. No one can know whether Paul would have disapproved of the practice of same-sex intercourse by a Christian who (a) had a relatively exclusive and fixed homosexual orientation; (b) experienced a deep personal dissatisfaction with celibacy; and (c) acted in the context of a loving and committed "life partnership" (pp. 19, 31, 34-35).

3. To insist on an absolute ban of all homosexual relationships is to "fly in the face of Scripture" because: (a) there are "thousands of homosexual Christians for whom neither therapy nor celibacy appears viable"; and (b) Genesis 2:18 allegedly tells us that it is God's will "for all people to have the opportunity of sharing life with a partner" (pp. 34, 36).

Given these intermediate suppositions, it is not surprising that Powell reaches the following conclusion: "I believe that . . . exceptions to the prohibited behavior must be granted in some instances to enable homosexual people to experience life as abundantly as possible" (p. 39). The gist of what he says previously more or less requires this belief. As we shall see, it is not so much Scripture as Powell's personal belief that shapes the three suppositions cited above.

II. What the church would be doing in granting exceptions

Powell begins the last section of his article by "clarifying what the Church would *not* be doing" if it sanctioned "some relationships between some homosexual persons who meet certain criteria defined by the Church (for instance, public commitment to a lifelong, monogamous union)." The Church, Powell claims, would not be: (1) "endorsing homosexuality as an alternative lifestyle," (2) "redefining marriage," (3) "condoning any specific sex acts," or (4) "discrediting the views or efforts of those who encourage celibacy or therapy as 'first options' for gay and lesbian persons" (pp. 36-37).

The full online[5] section shows that, if the church made thousands of so-called "exceptions" to a "usual policy" against homosexual behavior, it would indeed be doing all four things that Powell denies it would be doing. The term *exceptions* would become meaningless because the "usual policy" would apply only to those persons not particularly oriented toward violating it. On a pragmatic level, it would be impossible to know in advance of death what individuals might have an allegedly unalterable homosexual orientation. And what would count as an "exclusive" orientation when nearly all homosexuals experience some degree of heterosexual attraction at some point in life? What sense would it make to require a "public commitment to a lifelong, monogamous union" when no more than five percent of homosexual unions sanctioned by the church would turn out to be *both* lifelong *and* monogamous? It is also politically naïve to think that an initial acceptance of "exceptions" would not lead irresistibly to full acceptance. The church would necessarily redefine marriage. Even Powell makes his case for "exceptions" largely on the basis of an appeal to the Bible's key marriage text: Genesis 2:18-24. The alternative to such a redefinition is to institutionalize sex outside of marriage. The church will also have to turn a blind eye to the practices that typify homosexual relationships. Certainly, too, a powerful homosexual lobby in the church is not going to accept any policy on celibacy or therapy as "first options" for homosexuals. In fact, a policy of "exceptions" would embolden prohomosex forces to coercive indoctrination and intimidation in order to stamp out any last vestiges of "prejudice" against same-sex intercourse. Any remaining holdouts in the church would be treated as the moral equivalent of racists and disciplined accordingly. Incidentally, a plan for "local option" would produce the same adverse effects as a plan for "exceptions."

III. Interpretive issues: core values, structural complementarity, and the burden of proof

In the full online[6] section, I discuss the criteria for determining what constitutes a core value for Scripture: a value that is pervasively, strongly, and absolutely held in opposition to broader cultural trends. Such a value is the heterosexual ("other-sexual") prerequisite for sexual unions. That Powell could justify exceptions to Scripture's prohibition of homosexual practice by an appeal to Jesus' interpretation of Sabbath law shows how much Powell underestimates the significance of this prerequisite.

The Bible's prohibition of incest, and particularly sex with one's mother, provides the closest analogue to the prohibition of same-sex intercourse. It illustrates the utter gravity of maintaining minimum standards for structural complementarity in sexual mergers. Powell's discussion of "the gift of sexuality," focusing as it does on durable intimacy, overlooks this crucial dimension (p. 21). "Sexual orientation" does not take precedence over the matter of too much structural identity. Surely Powell would not want to sanction a man-mother union even if there were an "orientation" involved.

Powell rightly states that anyone who wants to argue for exceptions to Scripture's prohibition of same-sex intercourse has to meet a "heavy burden of proof" (pp. 28, 35). Doesn't this require Powell to *assume*, apart from unambiguous historical evidence to the contrary, that Paul would not have made any exceptions for "the redeemed Christian who continues to have homosexual impulses or to engage in homosexual activity that is neither promiscuous nor exploitative" (p. 31)? As it is, Powell argues for exceptions without having supplied such evidence.

IV. The male-female prerequisite in the Genesis creation stories
A. Powell's reading of Genesis 2:18-24

Powell does not dismiss the significance of Genesis 2:18-24 for the procomplementarity side of the discussion. However, he truncates its value for a "procomp" position while using it as the key proof text for promoting exceptions consistent with a prohomosex perspective. According to Powell (pp. 21, 29, 32), Genesis 2:18-25 tells us that:

(1) God designed humans at creation for heterosexual relations.

(2) *But* this design is only the "normal state of affairs."

(3) Homosexual relations are a departure from God's design.

(4) *But* homosexual relations are not necessarily sinful.

(5) All references to homosexual acts in the Bible are negative.

(6) *But* God declares that it is "not good" for humans to be alone. It is God's will that all people have the opportunity of being in a sexually intimate, lifelong partnership with another person.

In this point-counterpoint presentation of Genesis 2:18-25, I would identify points (1), (3), and (5) as accurate, but points (2), (4), and (6) as either misleading or inaccurate. The best way of showing this is simply to give my own understanding of the import of the Genesis creation stories and then come back and explain where my understanding differs from that of Powell.

B. The male-female prerequisite in Genesis 1:26-28

Let us begin with Genesis 1:26-28 which, surprisingly, gets almost no play in Powell's article (N1).

> [26]And God said, "Let us make an *adam* (an earthling, humankind, man) in our image, in accordance with our likeness, and let them have dominion over the fish . . . birds . . . cattle . . . wild animals. . . and over every crawling thing that crawls on the earth."
> [27]**And God created the *adam* in his image,**
>   **in the image of God he created it (or: him),**
>   **male and female he created them.**
> [28]And God blessed them and God said to them, "**Be fruitful and multiply** and fill the earth and subdue it and have dominion over the fish...the birds...and every living thing that crawls on the earth."

What does this text contribute to a discussion of the Bible and homosexual practice? I see at least four points here.

1. Genesis 1:27 brings into close connection creation "in God's image" and creation as "male and female." *If* sex is to be had, the image of

God manifests itself in a complementary male-female union. This is different from asserting that individuals *must* engage in sexual intercourse in order to manifest God's image. Rather, there are ways of having sex that would efface the image of God stamped on humans and ways of having sex that would enhance that image. The former would include bestiality, same-sex intercourse, and adultery; the latter — certainly in Jesus' understanding of this text (Mark 10:6-9) — lifelong monogamous unions with someone of the opposite sex. In the sexual dimension of life humans are "angled" or "faceted" expressions of the image and likeness of God, "male and female." They have integrity or wholeness as God's image, independent of sexual activity. Yet, when they engage in sexual activity, they engage another in their particularity, as only one incomplete part of a two-faceted sexual whole. Ignoring this particularity effaces that part of the divine image stamped on human sexuality.

2. One such complementary dimension concerns the capacity to procreate, though it is not likely that the narrator limited complementarity to this one function. For example, the idea that P would have viewed an infertile male-female sexual union as the moral equivalent of a homoerotic union is, from the vantage point of historical-critical study, preposterous. It is worth noting also that Jesus interpreted the creation of male and female in Genesis 1:27 as the basis not merely for procreative acts but also for the entire holistic joining of two into one flesh (Gen 2:24).

3. The narrator of Genesis 1 gives special attention to issues of structural compatibility, specifically to ordering according to various "kinds" (vv. 11-12, 21, 24-25; *cf.* 6:20; 7:14; N2). Such attention precludes any openness on the narrator's part toward same-sex intercourse.

4. The story of the human creation in Genesis 1:26-31 stresses compatibility, not male dominance. "Male and female" *combined* express God's image. Both are commanded to manage God's creation (N3).

C. The male-female prerequisite in Genesis 2:18-24

Genesis 2:18-24 brings the male-female requirement into even sharper relief than Genesis 1:26-28.

> [18]And Yahweh God said, "It is not good for the *adam* to be alone; I will make for him a helper as his counterpart (*ezer kenegdo*)." [19]And Yahweh God formed from the ground (*adamah*) every animal of the field and every bird of the air, and brought them to the *adam* . . . [20] but for the *adam* there was not found a helper as his counterpart.
>
> [21]And **Yahweh God** caused a deep sleep to fall upon the *adam*, and he slept; and he **took one of his sides** (or: ribs) and closed up its place

with flesh. **²²And Yahweh God built the side** (or: rib, *tsela*) **that he had taken from the *adam* into a woman** and brought her to the *adam*.

²³And the *adam* said, "This at last is bone from my bones and flesh from my flesh; to this one shall be given the name 'woman' (*ishshah*) for from man (*ish*) this one was taken."

²⁴Therefore a man (*ish*) shall leave his father and his mother and become attached (or: joined, united) **to his woman/wife (*ishshah*) and the two shall become one flesh.**

What is the image here? The term *tsela*, traditionally rendered "rib," is nowhere else used of part of the human body. Normally, it denotes the "side" of an object. Of note is the interpretation of Rabbi Samuel bar Nahman (third century A.D.):

> "When God created Adam, he created him facing both ways; then he sawed him in two and made two backs, one for each figure."
> (*Genesis Rabbah* 8:1)

The image presented in Genesis 2:21-22 appears to be that of an originally binary human, or one sexually undifferentiated, who is split down the side to form two sexually differentiated counterparts. Marriage is pictured as a *reconstitution* of the two constituent parts, male and female, that were the products of the splitting.

In this depiction same-sex erotic unions are precluded as a matter of course. Why? The reason is that the only differentiation created by the splitting is the two sexes, male and female. Accordingly, the most essential requirement of human sexual relations — the only one that restores the original sexual unity — is that there be a male and a female to effect this *re*-union. "Becoming one flesh" is not just about intimacy, romance, raising a family, and generally sharing one's life with another in a lifelong union (*contra* Powell). Yes, it is those things but it also more: It is about *re*uniting male and female into a sexual whole. This *re*union cannot come about artificially, that is, through the contorted gender nonconformity of one or the other partner. Rather, it transpires truly, by means of the *re*merging of divided constituent parts: essential male and essential female. Neither party need, or can, compromise gender integrity to effect the *re*union. God specifically designed men and women for a holistic fittedness in terms of anatomy, physiology, distinctive stimulation patterns, and relational expectations. A same-sex sexual partner does not supply the missing sexual complement, no matter how hard he or she tries. Authorization of homoerotic unions requires a different kind of creation account — something like the comical story of human origins spun by Aristophanes in Plato's *Symposium* (189C-193D), in which an original man-male, female-female, and male-female are each split down the side and thereafter long for the other half (see N4 for a critique of Terence Fretheim's prohomosex reading of Genesis 2:18-25).

As with Genesis 1:26-28, Genesis 2:18-24 is not a text about keeping women down. It is not about misogyny. Adam yearns to rejoin, in one-flesh union, with his other half, his sexual "counterpart" and "helper."

D. "Men are from Mars, Women are from Venus"

Our brief review of the implications of the Genesis creation stories gives me boldness to go out on a limb and say: Men and women are different — significantly so (N5). That there is a widespread recognition of major male-female differences, not only in anatomy but also in a host of inter-personal dealings, is evident from the popularity of the slogan in the heading above.

An immediate and obvious example of sexual differentiation, apart from complementary anatomy and procreative function, arises in the area of sexual stimulation patterns. For example, the simple fact that women on average manufacture only about one-seventh the amount of the sex-hormone testosterone each day that men do accounts for significant differences between men and women, such as the intensity of the sex-drive and the kind and amount of interpersonal communication needed. Men are more visually stimulated, more genitally focused, and more easily aroused. In a classic psychological study that has been replicated many times over, male and female college students were recruited to approach persons of the opposite sex and ask, among other things, "Would you go to bed with me *tonight*?" Seventy-five percent of the males said "yes," as compared to none of the females. Among those of both sexes who responded "no," males tended to be apologetic while females were often offended (N7).

Of course, the great laboratory for examining male-female differences in action is the homosexual community (N8). In what ways does male homosexual behavior differ from female homosexual behavior? Relative to female homosexuals, male homosexuals have much higher rates of:

- Sex-partners
- "Open" unions
- Deviant sexual behavior, including: anal-oral contact, fisting, group sex, threesomes, bath-house encounters, prostitution, and anonymous sex
- Sexually transmitted disease

Even nonconformist homosexual men — flamboyantly effeminate men — tend to act, in the end, like men as regards patterns of sexual stimulation.

What about female homosexuality? On the whole women have higher, and more holistic, intimacy demands for sexual relationships. An example will illustrate. Soon after being married, an acquaintance of mine said to me, "Yesterday I washed and waxed the kitchen floor for my wife and later that night we had great lovemaking. Help me out here: What's the connection?" I assured him that his wife probably found nothing sexually arousing about Johnson Floor Wax. Rather, what aroused her was his concrete expression of care and concern for matters of interest to her. "But," he responded, "I don't need her to wax the floor to be aroused — unless, of course, she is doing it scantily clad." Exactly. Therein lays a qualitative and quantitative male-female difference. It is not a night-and-day difference. Men can be aroused by expressions of intimacy that go deeper than the mere sight of an attractive female body, just as women can be aroused by the appearance of the male body. It is a matter of degree and frequency. Similarly, there is probably a small percentage of men getting therapy for the fact that their wife does not communicate her innermost feelings often enough. For the vast majority of couples, however, communication problems are a recurring complaint of the woman. In the context of a relational give-and-take between a man and a woman, higher expectations for personal investment in the quality of the relationship, typically associated with the female partner, can have a salutary effect in deepening male commitment to the relationship. At the same time, the male temperament can moderate some unrealistic expectations in the female temperament and provide a healthy corrective to an over-identification of quality-of-relationship concerns with personal self-esteem. When the "masculine corrective" is absent, one gets the kind of problems that appear in female homosexual relationships: (1) relationships of slightly shorter duration than even male homosexual relationships, on average; and (2) a higher incidence of mental illness issues (e.g., bouts with depression) associated with relationship deficiencies or failures.

At this place of the discussion we are beginning to drift into negative side effects of homosexual behavior, which is hard not to do when one talks about why homosexual practice is wrong. My main points, however, are:

- Man and woman complement each other sexually.
- Holiness in sex is not just about separation: it is about completion and wholeness.
- There is something wrong when a person perceives union with a sexual same as completion of the sexual self. The integrity of the sexual

self is denied. Sexual gaps are not filled and the extremes of each sex are not moderated.

There is a great irony in the propaganda put out by pro-homosex advocacy groups. On the one hand, they often deny the significance of sexual differentiation for purposes of mate selection: What does it matter, they ask, if a person chooses a male sex-partner or a female sex-partner? On the other hand, homosexuals with a relatively exclusive attraction to members of the same sex tacitly affirm the significance of sexual differentiation. Why are "category 6" (exclusively homosexual) males not attracted, say, to "butch" females? Why are "category 6" females not attracted to effeminate men? Could there be something distinctively female and something distinctively male that transcend cultural stereotypes?

The bottom line is this: *Persons attracted to same sex are erotically stimulated by what they already are. This is sexual narcissism and/or self-deception.* It is a sexual desire either for one's self or for what one wishes to be but, in fact, already is. It is sin.

E. The Genesis prerequisite in canonical context

Confirmation for this structuralist reading of Genesis 1 and 2 (N9) comes from links elsewhere in the canon, particularly in (1) other texts from the same literary strands; and (2) reuse of Genesis 1:27 and 2:24 by Jesus and Paul.

1. *Relevant texts by the same narrator.* Literary critics generally agree that Genesis 2:18-24 belongs to the same source material ("J," from the "Yahwist") as the story of Sodom and Gomorrah (Gen 19:4-11) and the story of Ham's act against Noah (Gen 9:20-27). Like many, Powell dismisses the relevance of the Sodom narrative because it allegedly "speak[s] only of the sin of homosexual rape and say[s] nothing at all about consensual relations between persons of the same sex" (p. 23).

But how does one know this? The narrative does not tell us that the male-male dimension of the attempted rape had nothing to do with the particular heinousness of the actions of the Sodomite men. The same narrator tells an analogous story in Ham's act against Noah. Many (e.g., von Rad, Nissinen, Wold, myself) have made a case that this story is about Ham's *rape* of his father (N10). For illustrative purposes, let us assume for the moment that this is a correct interpretation. Would anyone want to argue that Genesis 9:20-27 "speaks only of the sin of incestuous rape and says nothing at all about consensual relations between a man and his father?" Obviously such a conclusion would be preposterous. The incestuous dimension, to say nothing of the dimension of same-sex intercourse, clearly ratchets up the dimension of depravity for this ancestor of the Canaanites. Incest is wrong regardless of whether it is coerced or consensual. In short, Genesis 9:20-27 is a "kitchen sink" story of ultimate Canaanite depravity. The ancestor of the Canaanites not only commits rape but rape of one of his parents (incest), and not only so but also rape of his same-sex parent, his father (same-sex intercourse). It is not mere coincidence that Leviticus 18 opens and ends its list of sex-laws (incest, male-male intercourse, etc.) with a warning not to commit the same sexual offenses that the Canaanites had committed. Sex with one's parent is always wrong because it is sexual relations with "the flesh of one's flesh" (18:6). Male-male intercourse is always wrong because it entails — in Powell's own words — "doing something with another man that ought properly be done with a woman" (p. 24).

The Sodom narrative is another "kitchen sink" story of Canaanite depravity: not just rape, but gang-rape as severe in hospitality to travelers seeking temporary lodging; and not just this but treating males not as males but as though they were females with an orifice for male penetration. That male-male intercourse per se is a significant compounding factor in the story is evident from many considerations:

- The Yahwist's story of Ham in Genesis 9:20-27, with its ideological link to Leviticus 18.
- The Yahwist's story of the creation of woman in Genesis 2:18-24 and its clear portrayal of woman as the one and only sexual "counterpart" for man.
- The probable anti-homosex interpretations of the Sodom story in Ezekiel 16:49-50 (Ezekiel interprets the Sodom narrative through the lens of Holiness Code or something very much like it) and in Jude 7 and 2 Peter 2:7, 10 (N11), to say nothing of a number of anti-homosex interpretations in early Judaism.
- The parallel story of the Levite at Gibeah in Judges 19:22-25, told by a narrator (the "Deuteronomistic Historian") who elsewhere abhors the receptive homoerotic associations of the qedeshim ("homosexual cult prostitutes") .
- The ancient Near Eastern context, which often disparages males who willingly play the role of females in sexual intercourse.
- The implications of the rest of the Old Testament canon, which in any material dealing with sexual relations always presumes the sole and exclusive legitimacy of heterosexual unions.

For the documentation behind the claims made above, I refer readers to other works of mine (N12). In short, if the Sodom narrative is read contextually — that is, with historical and literary contexts in view — there can be little doubt that this narrative, along with several other Old Testament texts, rejects all male-male intercourse on the grounds of structural discomplementarity. For the narrator the difference between consent and coercion is the difference between a man who willingly dishonors himself by serving as the sexual counterpart to another male and a man who is forcibly dishonored by others.

Coming from the same literary source, the creation story in Genesis 2:18-24 and the Sodom/Ham narratives interpret each other. Genesis 2:18-24 suggests that the Sodom/Ham narratives were not condemning only coercive forms of same-sex intercourse. The Sodom/Ham narratives, in turn, suggest that the narrator of Genesis 2:18-24 really did intend the story to have negative implications for same-sex intercourse.

I have not said anything yet about literary connections with Genesis 1:26-28, commonly identified as the work of the "Priestly Writers" (P). The relationship between P and H (the Holiness Code, Leviticus 17-26) is not clear; but if, as many think, P absorbed H (N13), then P undoubtedly accepted the prohibition of male-male intercourse in Leviticus 18 and 20. Even if the literary relationship between the two works was different, a person would be hard pressed to make a case for any openness on P's part to homosexual activity, given P's obvious structuralist tendencies. Certainly, too, the final canonical shaping of the Pentateuch leaves no doubt about the implications of Genesis 1:26-28 for all same-sex intercourse.

2. *Jesus and Paul on the male-female prerequisite in creation.* I will treat Paul in more detail in the next section. Suffice it to say here that lying in the background of Paul's critique of same-sex intercourse in Romans 1:24-27 and 1 Corinthians 6:9 are, respectively, Genesis 1:27 (an intertextual echo) and Genesis 2:24 (explicitly cited in close contextual proximity). Paul understood these two key creation texts to contain an implicit proscriptive component. In establishing that a holistic sexual union requires the remerging of man and woman, the creation texts necessarily proscribe all homoerotic relationships.

What of Jesus? According to Mark 10:2-12, Jesus addressed a question about human sexuality by appealing to Genesis 1:27 and 2:24. It is probably not mere coincidence that both Jesus and Paul latched onto these same two texts as having ultimate significance for defining sexual morality.

> [2]And when Pharisees approached, they were asking him if it was permissible for a man to divorce his wife, testing him. [3]And in response he said to them: "What did Moses command you?" [4]And they said: "Moses allowed to write a certificate of divorce and to divorce."

⁵But Jesus said to them: "With a view to your hardness of heart he wrote to you this command. ⁶**But from the beginning of creation, '*male and female he made them*'** (Gen 1:27). ⁷'*For this reason a man will leave his father and mother and will be joined to his wife,* ⁸*and the two will become one flesh*'** (Gen 2:24). So they are no longer two but one flesh. "What then God has yoked together, let no man separate."

The following points can be culled from this account:

(1) Jesus regarded Genesis 1:27 and 2:24 as normative for defining sexual practice; as prescriptive, not just descriptive. Indeed, Jesus viewed God's will for human sexuality expressed in Genesis 1-2 as having precedence over any subsequent watering down of the Creator's will, even in the Mosaic law. Thus, the concession to male hardness of heart given by Moses — allowance of a male right to divorce — is revoked in favor of the more stringent sex ethical demand implicitly established at creation. Jesus was so intent on prioritizing sexual purity over other considerations that he even declared that a man marrying a divorced woman committed adultery (so the parallel texts in Luke 16:18 and Matthew 5:32; *cf.* 1 Corinthians 7:10-11).

(2) Although Jesus focused on the indissolubility of marriage, he *presupposed* as the one essential prerequisite that there be a "male and female." Only a "man" and a "woman" are structurally capable of becoming "one flesh" through a sexual union. Of note is the interesting back-to-back linking of Genesis 1:27 and 2:24, giving the impression that Jesus understood the "for this reason" introducing 2:24 as alluding to the gender differentiation established in 1:27. "*For this reason* — namely, because God made them male and female, complementary sexual beings (1:27) — man and woman may be joined in a permanent one-flesh union (2:24).

(3) For Jesus, then, the Creator ordained marriage — it is not just a social construct — as a lifelong union of one man and one woman for the purpose of forming an indissoluble sexual whole. Both the Scriptures that Jesus cited with approval and the audience that Jesus addressed — indeed the whole of early Judaism so far as extant evidence indicates — presumed the male-female prerequisite. Jesus clearly agreed.

(4) When Jesus cited Genesis 1:27 and Genesis 2:24 to address the issue of divorce, he was not divesting them of their implicit proscription of all homoerotic behavior. He was narrowing further an already narrowly defined understanding of normative sexuality, drawn in part from these creation stories, to mandate the indissoluble character of marriage as well. Another area where he intensified demands for lifelong monogamy was the human heart (so the adultery of the heart say-

ing in Matthew 5:27-28). Jesus was not making lifelong monogamy a more important consideration for sexual relations than the heterosexual dimension. The latter remained for Jesus the unshakeable prime prerequisite for all considerations of fidelity and longevity. Certainly no reasonable person would argue that Jesus prioritized monogamy and permanence over the intra-human and non-incestuous character of normative sexual relationships. Because Jesus' conviction about a male-female prerequisite at creation was shared throughout early Judaism (N14), he could focus on other facets of sexual relationships over which disputes existed in his cultural context (N15).

F. Implications for Powell's view

We began this section noting that Powell was on target in some remarks about Genesis 2:18-24 and considerably off-target in others. It is now time to expand on these observations.

1. *A prerequisite, not just the "normal state of affairs."* It is not enough to label the other-sexual character of sexual relations in Genesis 1-2 as *the normal state of affairs*. It is a *prerequisite*.

To his credit, Powell stretches the usual meaning of *normal state of affairs* to encompass the notion of God's intent and design at creation — which, in turn, should have led him to drop the weak word *normal* altogether. In the strongest statement of his essay he even goes so far as to say that "the Bible appears to indicate that [intimate, becoming-one] bonds are to be formed between men and women, not between two men or between two women"; and that "homosexual relations are regarded as a departure from God's design" (p. 32). Most people, I think, would understand these statements to mean that homosexual activity is always (necessarily, intrinsically) sinful and thus never to be *approved* under any circumstances.

Yet this is not what Powell means. In his next-to-last summary of the Bible's position he refers to "the biblical perspective . . . that presents *homosexual behavior* as activity that is *normally* contrary to God's will" (p. 36; emphasis mine). This statement is inaccurate. The perspective of Genesis 1-2 — certainly in the view of the narrators and in the view of Jesus and Paul — is that homosexual relations are *always* contrary to God's will because they always violate the heterosexual *prerequisite* for sexual relations established at creation.

In his last summary of the Bible's position Powell states, "The Bible regards the instances of same-sex intercourse *to which it refers* as shameful and degrading acts, unacceptable conduct for God's people" (p. 37; emphasis mine). The clause "to which it refers" indicates a potential limit on the Bible's opposition to same-sex intercourse. The following statement, introduced by "on the other hand," presses on that limitation by insisting that God wants homosexual persons to have a "life-partner." However, the creation texts do not provide Powell with a limitation on the mandatory character of the male-female dimension of sexual relations. The male-female requirement is unconditional. Same-sex erotic unions are precluded as a matter of course because the rejoining effected by a sexually intimate bond requires the constituent parts of the splitting: man and woman.

Powell seems to present the male-female prerequisite as an *ideal* for human sexuality (*cf.* p. 35). That is not enough. The attempt to remerge into a sexual whole two persons who are structurally discordant for such a re-merger seriously distorts the gender integrity of the two participants. Sexual intercourse is only for sexual counterparts. Whether or not the participants know it, homoerotic intercourse makes a statement that the participants find sexual completion in one another. The Bible always regards sexual mergers that violate structural prerequisites as extremely serious violations of God's design in creation (man-mother sex and human-animal sex are cases in point). Apart from the requirement that humans limit their sexual mergers to other humans, there is no more basic, or sacred, expectation placed on human sexual activity than the male-female prerequisite. Scripture regards its violation as the ultimate sacrilege against God's design of male and female.

Where Powell gets lost a bit, and might lose his readers, is in his characterization of *heterosexual relationships* as the normal state of affairs (pp. 21, 29, 32). Technically, this is a true statement, so long as one means only that not everyone will enter a sexual relationship. But in the context of discussing the perspective of Genesis 1-2 on homosexual relations it is imprecise and misleading because it does not encapsulate *everything* that the creation texts affirm. Powell thinks that saying "homosexual behavior . . . is normally contrary to God's will" is the flipside of saying that heterosexual relationships are the normal state of affairs. It is not. The latter statement leaves the door open for celibacy, consistent with the biblical perspective; the former requires the conclusion that homosexual relationships are not wrong in all circumstances, inconsistent with the biblical perspective. From a biblical point of view, although it is technically true to say that same-sex intercourse is contrary to the normal state of affairs, it is technically false to claim that same-sex intercourse is contrary *only* to the normal state of affairs. Same-sex intercourse is contrary *also* to the heterosexual prerequisite for sexual relationships. As such it is *always* contrary to God's will, not just *normally* so.

Any number of analogies would make this clear. If an article came out saying that man-mother sex, human-animal sex, or sex with a prepubescent child was contrary to the normal state of affairs, critics would rightly jump all over that claim — not because the claim would be technically false but because it would be false in a *performative* sense. It would imply that man-mother sex, human-animal sex, or sex with a prepubescent child was contrary *only* to the normal state of affairs and not necessarily contrary to an absolute prohibition. In not saying enough, the statement would grant license to claims for exceptions and erode resistance to the behavior in general. It would deserve to be condemned as irresponsible.

For this reason Powell's attempt to justify the expression *normal state of affairs* by appealing to other variations of the creation paradigm — celibacy and childlessness — does not work (pp. 21-22). The Bible does not declare celibacy and childlessness to be sin. However, *if sex is to be had*, there are ways of having it that the Bible considers necessarily sinful, and egregiously so. The other two variations from the creation paradigm that Powell cites, polygamy and divorce, are unlike same-sex intercourse in that they are (a) permitted under exceptional circumstances in the Old Testament and, as regards divorce, in the New Testament as well; and, (b) following from this point, were/are not regarded as unnatural acts, at least not on the order of same-sex intercourse. Even given these ameliorating factors, which make polygamy and divorce much less serious offenses than same-sex intercourse, the church today takes a very dim view of repeat offenses. Indeed, it permits no exceptions as regards any form of "plural marriage" in Western culture. Even in third world cultures where polygamy is an accepted practice the church disallows new wives and encourages disengagement from extra wives when children are not involved. As for divorce, the church takes a dim view of even one divorce, to say nothing of multiple divorces. A homoerotic union, however, involves numerous immoral, proactive, and unnatural sexual acts over a long term and without regard for the necessity of repentance.

As we argued in section III, the closest analogy to same-sex intercourse is incest and the particularly extreme form of man-mother incest. There are no exceptions here, not even hypothetical ones. The level of structural sacrilege is too high for any exceptions to be entertained and for any reason.

2. *A sexual complement*, *not just an "intimate life-partner."* Powell uses another expression that obscures the witness of the creation texts, "intimate life-partner," which he identifies with the quality of "becoming one" in Genesis 2:24 (N16). For example, from pp. 32, 34, 36, 37, and 38 (emphasis mine):

> The Bible teaches that it is the will of God for all people to have the opportunity of *sharing life with a partner*, a person with whom they form *an intimate bond so as to "become one."*

> Thousands of homosexual Christians for whom neither therapy nor celibacy appear to be viable options. . . . experience what Paul calls "burning" for a *life-partner*.

> The Bible does indicate . . . that it is God's will for individuals to have the opportunity of *sharing their lives with intimate partners* (Gen. 2:18-25). The Church may set limits regarding such partnerships . . . but to insist on limits that deny thousands of people the possibility of such relationships altogether is to fly in the face of scripture.

> God does not want homosexual persons (or anyone else) to have to live alone, denied the opportunity of *"becoming one" with a life-partner through an intimate bond* of love and devotion.

> Do we require homosexual people to sacrifice the experience of *sharing life intimately with a partner* in order to fulfill God's standards of holiness as perfectly as possible?

Genesis 1:27 and 2:24 do affirm that sexual intimacy, partnership, and lifelong commitment are essential ingredients of the bond described therein. But Genesis 2:18-24 puts forward a much bigger idea, that of a sexual "counterpart," a being "taken from man" that is man's *sexual complement*. This is *the* essential element in a sexual union where two "become one flesh." By stripping this aspect of "becoming one flesh" through use of the generic descriptor, "intimate life-partner," Powell is able to raise the possibility of a homosexual partnership "approximating the sort of intimate (normally heterosexual) bond that God willed to be a part of human experience" (p. 37). If, instead, Powell had replaced every occurrence of "intimate life-partner" and the like with "lifelong sexual complement of one's own," all talk of a homosexual approximation of the heterosexual bond would have been precluded from the start. The extent to which Powell does not view the reconstitution of male and female into a sexual whole as the central, indispensable feature of "becoming one flesh" is the extent to which Powell deviates from Genesis 2:18-24. There can be no exceptions to the male-female dimension of sexual relations because it is one of the two most vital considerations (N18).

3. *A conditional opportunity for sexual intimacy, not an opportunity by right.* Powell uses Genesis 2:18, "it is not good for the human to be alone," as a crowbar to pry exceptions, at least potentially, from Scripture's absolute prohibition of same-sex intercourse. His main premise, based on his interpretation of Genesis 2:18, appears in the first quotation cited in point 2 above. The church "requires" homosexuals, "for whom neither therapy nor celibacy appears viable," to be celibate (pp. 31-32, 34, 38). Celibacy, in turn, "if required, will render many people's lives 'not good' in the eyes of God" (ibid.). This, Powell thinks, compels the church to reconsider the possibility of exceptions and, so far as Powell's personal view is concerned, to mandate exceptions. I have six problems with this reading of Genesis 2:18.

First, as noted in points 1 and 2, *if* Genesis 2:18-24 can be said to give all persons an *opportunity* for a sexual relationship, that opportunity must be defined as an opportunity to have a lifelong sexual complement of one's own. Genesis 2:18-24 does not give anyone an opportunity — in Powell's use the term seems to border on the meaning of an inalienable God-given *right* — to have a generic "life-partner" minus an other-sex prerequisite. In other words, this is at best a *conditional opportunity* for a sexual relationship. A "homosexual orientation," which is already a sign of disordered sexuality, does not alter the prerequisite for a sexual complement. Indeed, without a sexual complement, it is not even possible, let alone allowable, for two persons of the same sex to become "one flesh" through a sexually intimate relationship. Sexual wholeness depends entirely on having two sexes. A sexual merger is precluded *on a structural level*, as are man-mother and human-animal sexual unions. Despite broader cultural trends to the contrary, the narrators of Genesis 1-2 and later interpreters such as Jesus and Paul disallowed all sexually intimate unions that did not have the sexual reunion of male and female as a prime objective. In short, if there is an opportunity for all, it is an opportunity that must first meet certain structural prerequisites. Sex or gender is one; number of partners, the term of commitment, and age are others — irrespective of whether the participants are "oriented" toward opposite-sex partners, monogamy, longevity, and sex with an adult. A complete loss of sexual interest can develop from many factors, not just the sex or gender of one's partner. If people are unhappy with God's conditional provision, they do not get to choose whatever option brings satisfaction to their sexual desires.

Second, there are different senses and degrees to a phrase like "not good." While it is "not good" for humans to be alone, it is far *worse* for humans to engage in same-sex intercourse. The former is not a sin but an experience of deprivation. The latter is regarded by Scripture as a violation of a core value in sexual ethics. To engage in same-sex intercourse as a means of averting loneliness is to subvert a higher value in Scripture for the sake of a lesser consideration. By the same token, to engage in one of the severest forms of sexual immorality (same-sex intercourse) as a means of avoiding additional sexual immoralities is, to put it bluntly, perverse. In my estimate, Powell seriously underestimates the degree to which Scripture regards the heterosexual dimension as a priority or, conversely, considers homoerotic intercourse per se as a high offense.

Third, Powell seems to assume that the *only* provision made by God to keep humans from being alone is the possibility of a committed sexual relationship with another person. But in the context of Genesis 2:18-25 there are no other humans. So obviously the first, and for a time only, provision to combat loneliness is the creation of a sexual counterpart for a sexually intimate union. Thereafter, however, the aloneness experienced by humans is partly alleviated through populating the world with offspring. There is also a strong stress in the New Testament on the church as the new family of believers. In short, the phrase "not good" and its linkage to the solution in 2:24 is, to a significant degree, conditioned by the special circumstance that there is no other human with whom the earthling is to have fellowship. In the scope of Scripture's entirety, "becoming one flesh" with a sexual counterpart is far from God's only answer to the problem of being alone, even if it is *a* significant answer.

Fourth, there are no guarantees in life that one will find a sexually satisfying marriage partner, let alone that one will live in marital bliss and harmony. Some do, but many who would like to — including a larger number of heterosexuals than homosexuals — do not. Every sexual rule risks denying a sexually "intimate lifetime partnership" to some group of people. The rule against same-sex intercourse is no exception. The alternative to such rules is sexual libertinism.

Fifth, Powell argues:

> But there are significant differences between (a) an individual who chooses to live as a single person, (b) an individual who would prefer not to live as a single person but who is unable to find a partner, and (c) an individual who is *required* to live alone when otherwise he or she would find the partner he or she desires. (p. 31)

I have four problems with this argument. (1) No person is *required* to live alone. All people are required to conform their sexual desires and relationships to the standards operative for the new covenant set down in Scripture. (2) As we noted earlier, no given homosexual Christian can predict that he or she will never experience any heterosexual arousal. Indeed, in the vast majority of cases some experience of heterosexual arousal for those who self-identify as homosexual is the norm. (3) There is no significant *existential* difference between (a) a heterosexual Christian who, in seeking to be faithful to the Lord, has not found a much desired "intimate life partner" (spouse) and (b) a homosexual Christian who, in exercising similar fidelity, is bereft of the same. (4) As suggested above, close intimate friendships — the *koinonia* or "partnership" with fellow believers — must always be kept in view as a counterweight to individual loneliness. It is not necessary to have sex with persons to be bonded to them. A classic case in point is Jonathan and David.

Sixth, I cannot agree with Powell's statement that "the Church must think carefully about whether it really wants to require [gay and lesbian] people to live in a manner that its Scriptures and its confessions maintain is *displeasing to God*" (p. 31; my emphasis). This way of formulating the matter is too one-sided and bleak. Singleness, even when experienced as a difficult deprivation, is not a sin; engaging in same-sex intercourse is. God is always *pleased* with someone who is obedient in hard times and *displeased* with those who live in disobedience. Life cannot be lived this side of the *eschaton* without some sense of deprivation and deep loss. Indeed, Christ himself called on those who would follow him to deny themselves, take up their cross, and lose their life for his sake (Mark 8:34-37). How can Christians who are denying themselves out of obedience to Jesus be living lives "displeasing to God"? Refraining from homosexual behavior, not participating in it, is pleasing to God.

Paul pleaded with God to remove his "thorn in the flesh" (cataracts?), only to discover that God's grace was sufficient for him, that God's power is perfected in his weakness (2 Corinthians 12:8-9). This was only one of numerous hardships faced by Paul in the course of his apostolic ministry (11:23-29). Yet he had learned to boast of his weaknesses "that the power of Christ may rest upon me" (12:9) and to be content in all circumstances, knowing that he could do all things through the One who strengthened him (12:10; *cf.* Philippians 4:11-12). God is ultimately pleased with forming Christ in us, often by making use of adverse circumstances. It is all too easy for us to lose sight of the "eternal weight of glory beyond all measure" that awaits us (2 Corinthians 4:17). Yes, the church should do what it can to help those experiencing deprivation — but always short of violating God's commands. The church should continue working toward meeting the intimacy needs of heterosexuals and homosexuals alike without abandoning the core sexual standards of Scripture.

V. The rest of the case for regarding same-sex intercourse as intrinsically sinful

The male-female prerequisite established in the Genesis creation stories cinches the point that the Bible presents same-sex intercourse not only as intrinsically unnatural but also as intrinsically sinful. However, so that there is no chance of resurrecting the allegedly biblical allowance of exceptions, we continue with the rest of the case.

A. The Levitical prohibitions

As Powell himself argues, the Levitical prohibitions are opposed to male-male intercourse because male-male intercourse "involves a man doing something with another man that ought properly be done with a woman. This thought seems consistent with the perspective of the creation story" (p. 24). What is that something? "Lying with," i.e., a euphemism for "having sexual intercourse with." Now, what exceptional case of sex between males could one cite that would fly under the radar of these proscriptions? The only "exception" would be a case of sex between males that did not involve sex between males — a complete oxymoron. Powell is right to acknowledge:

> That which is contrary to the normal state of affairs is not *necessarily* sinful, but the Holiness Code in the book of Leviticus indicates that homosexual activity is unnatural in a way that *is* sinful. Not everything in the Holiness Code applies to Christian morality, but Paul's apparent citation of the prohibitions against same-sex activity (through use of the word *arsenokoitai*) carries those commandments over into the New Testament in a way that *does* make them relevant. (p. 29; N19)

Let us lay out the logical consequences of this observation:

A. The Levitical prohibitions are absolute (without exception) as regards male-male intercourse. All such intercourse is necessarily (or intrinsically) sinful.

B. Paul's apparent citation of the prohibitions carries them over into the New Testament.

C. Conclusion: The New Testament regards same-sex intercourse as intrinsically sinful and thus as something to be prohibited absolutely — no exceptions (N20).

The conclusion is unassailable. Powell says that the prohibitions are made "relevant" by Paul's "apparent citation" but fails to draw the inevitable conclusion. His attempts at vitiating the force of this verdict in his discussion of *arsenokoitai* earlier in the article — "Still, the Church must be careful not to base moral teaching on an unsure interpretation of Scripture" (pp. 25-26) — are entirely unconvincing (see point 4 below) and, in the end, make the Levitical prohibitions *irrelevant* (N21). The Levitical prohibitions are only acknowledged as "relevant" if their view of male-male intercourse as intrinsically sinful is carried over into the interpretation of Paul's indictment of same-sex intercourse. Given that all Jews in antiquity, including Jesus and Paul, were to a considerable extent reliant on the Levitical proscriptions for their opposition to same-sex intercourse, it is inconceivable that Jesus and Paul would have made Powell's distinction between intrinsically unnatural and intrinsically sinful when the Levitical proscriptions made no such distinction. This one point, all by itself, is enough to sink Powell's contention that the Bible teaches that same-sex intercourse is just "normally contrary to God's will" (p. 36). But we proceed anyway.

B. The intertextual echo to Genesis 1:26-27 in Romans 1:23-27

In both Romans 1:24-27 and 1 Corinthians 6:9 there are intertextual echoes back to Genesis 1-2. With respect to Romans 1:24-27, the allusions are specifically to Genesis 1. The immediate context in Romans 1:20 and 1:25 explicitly mentions "the creation of the world" and "the Creator," respectively. Romans 1:23 transparently echoes Genesis 1:26:

> Let us make a *human* according to our *image* and . . . *likeness*; and let them rule over the . . . *birds* . . . and the *cattle* . . . and the *reptiles*. (Genesis 1:26)

> And they exchanged the glory of the immortal God for the *likeness* of the *image* of a mortal *human* and of *birds* and of *four-footed animals* and of *reptiles*. (Romans 1:23)

In such a context Paul's reference in Romans 1:26-27 to "females" having sex with females and "males" having sex with males, "contrary to nature" — that is, contrary to the material creation set in motion by the Creator and pronounced by God to be good — surely echoes Genesis 1:27: "male and female he made them." What is the point of these echoes to Genesis 1:26-27? Idolatry and same-sex intercourse — highlighted among an array of sins cited in Romans 1:18-32 — together constitute a frontal assault on the work of the Creator. Instead of humans recognizing their intermediate place between God, whom alone humans were to worship, and animals, over which humans were to rule, humans "worshipped and served the creation rather than the Creator" (Romans 1:25). Fittingly, God "handed over" those who did not honor him to self-dishonoring desires for sex with members of the same sex. Those who had suppressed "the truth about God" visible in creation/ nature (Romans 1:18-23, 25) would go on to suppress the truth about themselves visible in creation/nature, "committing indecency and receiving back among themselves the payback that was necessitated by their straying" from God (1:24, 26-27). For, though God "made them male and female" (Gen 1:27) for the purposes of sexual union and procreation (Gen 1:28), humans foolishly ignored the transparent complementarity of their sexuality by engaging in sex with the same sex and discrediting themselves. What is wrong, then, with same-sex intercourse, what makes it sinful, is that it does not correspond to the model of a male-female union given in these creation accounts (see N22 for a critique of Prof. David Fredrickson's denial of a link to Genesis).

Moreover, not only do the allusions to Genesis 1:26-27 make clear what Paul finds objectionable and sinful about same-sex intercourse but so do the explicit contrasts posed in the wording of Romans 1:26-27: females having sex with females rather than with males and males having sex with other males rather than with females. This makes it impossible to argue that there might be some form of homosexual behavior that would not be sinful in Paul's eyes. The only "exceptions" that Paul could possibly have allowed would be instances of male-male or female-female sexual intercourse between a man and a woman — again, a complete oxymoron.

C. The reference to nature in Romans 1:26-27

Powell rightly states that in Paul's understanding "*all* instances of homosexuality are unnatural." But he adds that for Paul only

> the instances of homosexuality known to his Roman readers are *both* unnatural *and* wrong. This still leaves open the possibility of some instances . . . in which homosexual relations could be regarded *only* as unnatural but *not* as wrong. (p. 28)

This argument is invalid. In Romans 1:24-27 Paul views same-sex intercourse as wrong precisely *because* it is contrary to nature. What is given as a supreme instance of "uncleanness" — a term for immoral sexual activity (N23), equated with sin in Romans 6:19 — and of "dishonorable" or "degrading passions" and of "indecency" is that "females exchanged the *natural* use for that which is *contrary to nature*, and likewise also the males, having left behind the *natural* use of the female, were inflamed with their yearning for one another, males with males." In other words, to exchange what is natural, defined as male-female intercourse, for that which is unnatural — female-female or male-male intercourse — is, in Paul's view, to engage in sinful, unclean, degrading, and indecent behavior. This sinful suppression of the truth about sexual design in nature parallels on the horizontal dimension the suppression of the truth about God in creation/nature that idolatry is on the vertical dimension.

So in this context it is impossible to say that only those instances "known to [Paul's] Roman readers are *both* unnatural *and* wrong" if "*all* instances of homosexual relations are unnatural" for Paul. Rather, one must say that if Paul regarded all instances of homosexual behavior as unnatural, then he regarded them all as wrong, for he deduces their wrongness, their sinfulness, from their character as actions contrary to nature. I do not know whether it is a slip on Powell's part or not, but he himself writes at one point: "Paul does not object to what he calls 'shameless acts' involving same-sex partners because they are promiscuous or exploitative; he specifically objects to them because they are 'unnatural'" (p. 27). If *unnatural* in this context does not necessarily mean *sinful*, then how could Paul base his objection to same-sex intercourse on its unnaturalness?

Furthermore, it will not do to argue, as Powell does, that actions can sometimes be contrary to (or beyond) nature without being sinful (p. 22). For the way in which the expression "contrary to nature" (*para phusin*) is employed *in the context of Romans 1:24-27* precludes a benign interpretation for this particular case (N24). Indeed whenever *para phusin* and like expressions appear in early Jewish literature *with reference to same-sex intercourse* they always constitute a basis for categorizing same-sex intercourse as a terrible sin (N25). In early Judeo-Christian understanding, some kinds of acts that are contrary to nature are *always* sinful (e.g., bestiality, sex with one's parent or child). That is exactly the case here. Same-sex intercourse was not regarded as a benign instance of acting beyond nature, like adoption. It was treated as a sinful rejection of the way in which God made male and female, as creations designed for a complementary, opposite-sex sexual relationship.

D. The evidence from 1 Corinthians 6:9

Powell allows that, as regards the vice list in 1 Corinthians 6:9,

> Paul might be viewed as carrying the prohibitions from
> Leviticus over into the New Testament, indicating that they
> *do* apply to Christians: sexual intercourse between two men is
> regarded as sinful and both the active (*arsenokoitai*) and passive
> (*malakoi*) participants in such activity need to repent. (p. 25)

Yet he then gives the following caution:

> Still, the Church must be careful not to base moral teaching
> on an unsure interpretation of Scripture. . . . First, it is pos-
> sible that the words are colloquial expressions referring to a
> particular type of homosexual conduct practiced in the first-
> century Corinthian culture. . . . Second, even if this is not true
> . . . these words are certainly not technical or scientific terms
> that necessarily describe *any* instance in which a man engages
> in sex with another man. . . . In short, the condemnations of
> *arsenokoitai* and *malakoi* in these texts may imply that *generally
> speaking*, men who have sex with other men are acting in a
> way that is not pleasing to God, but such condemnations do
> not disallow instances in which men who have sex with each
> other are *not* behaving as *arsenokoitai* or *malakoi*. (pp. 25-26)

I do not see how this can be possible.

1. *The Levitical connection.* The term *arsenokoitai* means "men who
lie with males" (N26). How can that not be inclusive, especially since it
is patterned on the Levitical prohibitions which Powell himself admits
are opposed to male-male intercourse on the grounds of what it is not:
male-female intercourse? If a man is supposed to have sex only with a
woman, what kind of male-male sexual union would not be covered?

2. *The Romans 1:24-27 connection.* Surely the best commentary on
what *arsenokoitai* would have meant for Paul, apart from Leviticus 18:22
and 20:13, appears in Romans 1:24-27 where Paul describes in the harsh-
est terms possible the wrong done whenever a male makes use of another male, rather than a female, as a partner in sexual intercourse. Given
this, plus the echo to Genesis 1:26-27 and the appeal to male-female
complementarity in nature, it is obvious that Paul — like the Levitical
prohibitions — is condemning every form of male-male intercourse in
Romans 1:27 and so in 1 Corinthians 6:9 as well. Like many pro-homosex
interpreters, Powell makes the mistake of discussing 1 Corinthians 6:9
in isolation from Romans 1:24-27.

3. *The incest connection in 1 Corinthians 5.* The vice list in 1 Corinthians 6:9-10 appears within a larger discussion of a case of incest (1 Corinthians 5). It is clear what Paul finds wrong with incest: the same thing that Leviticus finds wrong with incest. It is sex with one's own flesh (18:6); that is, sex with someone who is too much of a familial like. This is precisely what is *structurally* wrong with "men who lie with males": they are having sex with another who is too much of a like or same, here a person of the same sex, a gender same. If same-sex intercourse is wrong because it is sex between two non-complementary sexual sames, what kind of male-male sexual union could possibly be left out?

4. *The marriage connection in 1 Corinthians 7.* The chapter following the vice list is about marriage. In 1 Corinthians 7 Paul discusses only male-female sexual unions because these alone are valid. The presumption here, as everywhere in Scripture, is that sex is to be confined to male-female marriage. And if sex is to be confined to male-female marriage, what form of male-male sex could constitute a valid exception?

5. *The Genesis 2:24 connection in 1 Corinthians 6:12-20.* In the probably hypothetical example of a Christian resorting prostitutes in 1 Corinthians 6:12-20, Paul cites Genesis 2:24 (6:16). Clearly, in talking about sexual immorality, the standard set by the creation stories is Paul's own standard. The clause "the two shall become one flesh" obviously has in view the man who becomes joined to his woman/wife. What male-male attempt at creating a "one-flesh" union could possibly qualify when the re-merger requires a male and a female? To juxtapose *malakoi* and *arsenokoitai* with Genesis 2:24 is to remove any possibility that there might be "instances in which men who have sex with each other are not behaving as *arsenokoitai.*"

Given the above considerations, Powell is unconvincing when he claims that *arsenokoitai* and *malakoi* are imprecise, non-technical terms not necessarily embracing all forms of male-male intercourse. To be sure, Powell is right that several of the terms in the vice lists in 1 Corinthians 6:9-10 and 1 Timothy 1:9-10 may allow for some wiggle room in exceptional circumstances. Yet Powell cannot make this a universal rule. What persons who venerate the statues of foreign gods would Paul not have regarded as idolaters? What persons who have consensual sex with people other than their living spouse would not fall under the rubric of adulterers for Paul?

Powell latches onto the word *pornoi*, which he translates as "fornicators," and argues that there may be "exceptional circumstances in which sexual relations between persons who are not legally married might *not* be considered fornication" (p. 26). Later he cites the following example: "In remote locations where neither clergy nor legal magistrates are readily available, the Church has sometimes allowed committed couples to form sexual unions and bear children without taking part in a civil marriage service" (p. 35). Yet his example is a mere technicality. The church may allow such unions precisely because they do, in effect, constitute marriages. The Bible does not prescribe that clergy or legal magistrates officiate at a marriage ceremony. So their absence does not pose an insurmountable problem.

Moreover, *pornoi* here is a broader term than fornication. It means: "the sexually immoral." In 1 Corinthians 5 it includes participants in incest (vv. 9-11). The related abstract noun *porneia* is used of the act of soliciting prostitutes in 1 Corinthians 6:13, 18; indeed, the feminine personal noun, *porne*, properly refers to a "prostitute, harlot." With regard to the issue of prostitution discussed in 6:12-20, one might ask: are there exceptional circumstances of commercial sexual activity that the church would not consider prostitution and might therefore bless? I know of none. As for the case of incest in 1 Corinthians 5, although there is no single Greek (or Hebrew) word to describe a person having sex with his (step-) mother (N27), there are specific biblical prohibitions of it (Leviticus 18:7-8; 20:11; Deuteronomy 27:20), just as the reference to *arsenokoitai* relies on the prohibitions in Leviticus 18:22 and 20:13. In what exceptional circumstances might the church want to bless such unions? I suppose some sort of technicality would have to be raised by which one might argue that the woman in question is not one's mother or stepmother. What this technicality would be, I know not. Certainly Paul himself in 1 Corinthians 5 gives no indication that exceptions to the general rule might exist.

Since *arsenokoitai* is likely to have been patterned on the Levitical prohibitions of male-male intercourse, one would have to argue some technicality that would get around the all-inclusive character of those prohibitions. One would have to contend that the man seeking to have active intercourse with another male, or the male with whom he has intercourse, is not really a male (N28). What would justify such a contention? Certainly not the exceptions suggested by Powell; namely, exceptions for men of exclusive homoerotic orientation who commit themselves to monogamous lifelong unions. For such men do not cease to be men; nor do they claim to be other than men (N29). Similarly, one might ask with respect to the English term *bestiality*: are there any instances where a human having willful sex with an animal would not be a case

of bestiality? Again, one would have to argue on the basis of a technicality: either the human is not a human or the animal is not an animal.
Yet no such technicality could be persuasively presented.

Accordingly, we must contend against Powell that unless the
church can establish on the grounds of some clear technicality that the
participants in an alleged homoerotic encounter are not, in fact, members of the same sex, the church would have no legitimate basis for
circumventing 1 Corinthians 6:9 and 1 Timothy 1:10.

E. No great mystery: what Paul would have prescribed for the homo-sexual Christian in a committed homosexual union.

In an important paragraph at the end of p. 31 Powell discusses what
advice Paul might have given to a homosexual believer.

Powell begins by claiming, "It seems unlikely that Paul would
have counseled a homosexual believer simply to remain celibate" (N30).
Why would it seem unlikely? Even in 1 Corinthians 7 where he states
that husbands and wives should normally not deprive one another of
sexual intercourse "because of sexual immorality" (7:2-4), he commands
that "if in fact [a wife] is separated [from her husband], she should
remain unmarried or be reconciled with her husband" (7:11). Obviously
if Paul was willing to counsel divorced wives to remain unmarried unless they remarried their former husbands, how much more would he
have counseled believers with persistent and exclusive homoerotic desires to abstain from all sex with persons of the same sex? For the former
did not entail a form of unnatural sexual intercourse; the latter did.

Powell continues: "More likely, Paul would have hoped that the
sanctification of a believer . . . would replace [the 'degrading passions']
with natural yearnings that would allow for a normal, heterosexual marriage (Rom. 6:22; 1 Cor. 6:11)." Certainly Paul would have "hoped for"
this. We all hope for this. However, hoping for something and expect-
ing something as a matter of course are two very different things. Powell
may be contradicting himself at this point. For earlier in the article he
makes a point of arguing *against* those who cite 1 Corinthians 6:11 ("this
is what some of you used to be") as a proof text for the view that all
homosexuals can be transformed into heterosexuals. According to
Powell, 1 Corinthians 6:11 "seems to refer to changes in behavior rather
than to changes with regard to what some modern therapists call a
person's 'sexual orientation'" (p. 26). If Powell is right that 1 Corinthians
6:11 indicates that Paul expected a change in behavior rather than an
eradication of primary homoerotic impulses—and I believe Powell is

right — how can Powell subsequently argue that "we cannot know for certain what Paul would have prescribed for the redeemed Christian who continues to have homosexual impulses" (p. 31)? Powell's own reading of 1 Corinthians 6:11 indicates what Paul would have prescribed: Do not continue to engage in same-sex intercourse. You used to be a man who lies with males (or a woman who lies with a female). Stop being that kind of person. Change your behavior. You are no longer a slave to the sinful erotic desires for the same sex that may continue to exist in your bodily members.

Similarly, in Romans 6:19-21, Paul — while residing in Corinth — urged the believers at Rome not to be under the control of innate sinful passions:

> Just as you (viz., when you were unbelievers) presented your members as slaves to *uncleanness* and to lawlessness for lawlessness, so now (viz., as believers) present your members as slaves to righteousness for holiness. . . . For when you were slaves of sin, you were free with respect to righteousness. What fruit were you then having? Things of which you are now *ashamed*. For the end result of those things is *death*.

This is an obvious reference back to 1:24-27, where same-sex intercourse is singled out among sexual sins as a prime example of "uncleanness" and of "dishonorable passions" and "indecency," which along with other sins leads to death (1:32). *The very fact that Paul had to exhort believers not to return to such filthy conduct indicates the ongoing power of such impulses in their Christian lives.* By the same token, he believed that the Spirit made possible freedom from the dominant sway of all sinful impulses. The stakes were very high indeed:

> So then, brethren, we are debtors not to the flesh to live in conformity to the flesh (i.e., our sinful impulses), for if you live in conformity to the flesh, you are going to die; but if by the Spirit you are putting to death the deeds of the body, you will live. For as many as are being led by the Spirit, these are the sons of God. (Romans 8:12-14)

Paul certainly did not believe that becoming a Christian put an end to all strong temptations to have sex with someone of the opposite sex other than one's spouse; yet he could absolutely proscribe all prostitution, adultery, and (implicitly) polygamy and severely restrict the options for divorce and remarriage. As Paul told the Galatian believers,

> I say to you, walk by the Spirit and you will *not* carry out the desire of the flesh. For the flesh desires against the Spirit,

and the Spirit against the flesh, for these things are opposed to one another, that you may not do whatever you want. But if you are being led by the Spirit, you are not under the law. Now the works of the flesh are evident, which are sexual immorality, *uncleanness*, licentiousness. . . . [T]hose who serially do such things shall not inherit the kingdom of God. . . . Those who belong to Christ Jesus crucified the flesh with its passions and desires. If we live by the Spirit, let us also line up with (or: keep in step with) the Spirit. (Galatians 5:16-25)

Different sinful desires, sexual or otherwise, afflict different people at different rates of intensity. One person may have extraordinary difficulty in managing one kind of temptation, while another person may encounter difficulty in an entirely different area. Each person must subject his or her sinful desires to the Spirit's leading, die to self, and live for God. Those who struggle with intense homoerotic desires do not get an exemption. If it were otherwise, then there would be no point to any regulation of human behavior. In effect the message that would be sent is: "You do not have to obey this command if it turns out to be too hard for you." To proscribe homoerotic behavior absolutely only to those who do not experience intense homoerotic desires is no real proscription. Adultery and sex with prostitutes is proscribed equally to all alike, even though it is much harder for some people than for others to restrict sexual desire to one lifetime sex partner.

Powell claims that "we cannot know for certain what Paul would have prescribed for the redeemed Christian who continues to have homosexual impulses or to engage in homosexual activity that is neither promiscuous nor exploitative" (p. 31; N31). This claim stands in apparent contradiction to his admission that in Romans 1:26-27

Paul does not object to what he calls "shameless acts" involving same-sex partners because they are promiscuous or exploitative; he specifically objects to them because they are "unnatural." That verdict would seem to apply to all instances of sexual intercourse between same-sex partners, regardless of whether the sex was casual and regardless of whether prostitution or exploitation was involved. (p. 27)

Simply put, if promiscuity and exploitation are not the prime reasons for Paul's indictment of homosexual behavior, then there are no grounds for arguing that a non-promiscuous and non-exploitative homoerotic relationship would have changed Paul's indictment (N32). At the beginning of his article, Powell states:

Many Christians notice that no biblical text ever specifically comments on the morality of sexual relations between two men or two women who are in a loving relationship characterized by lifelong commitment. Thus, when two Christian men or women ask the Church to bless a relationship in which they will become romantic, spiritual, and probably sexual "life-partners," the Church is presented with a situation that never comes up, as such, in Scripture. (p. 19)

Such claims cannot be substantiated. Three points suffice to demonstrate this. First, the above observation is the equivalent of saying:

No biblical text ever specifically comments on the morality of sexual relations *between a mother and son or between two adult siblings* who are in a loving relationship characterized by lifelong commitment. Thus, when two Christian *nuclear-family members* ask the Church to bless a relationship in which they will become romantic, spiritual, and probably sexual "life-partners," the Church is presented with a situation that never comes up, as such, in Scripture.

Scripture does, in fact, address committed homoerotic unions, just as it addresses committed incestuous unions. It does so by taking up all possible forms under absolute proscriptions, making matters of commitment secondary to larger structural concerns such as prohibiting unions between people who are too much alike. Second, in the case of homoerotic unions, there is a distortion of gender itself since the logic of sexual intercourse necessarily converts one's same-sex partner into a sexual other. A homoerotic union characterized by fidelity and longevity does not alleviate this problem. Indeed, a lifelong relationship only exacerbates the problem by regularizing it, constantly conditioning the participants to image themselves in sexual union as complementary when in fact they are not. Third, the ancients were able to conceive of non-exploitative and non-promiscuous, lifelong loving relationships between two males; and such relationships also existed among lesbians (N33). Yet Jews and Christians in the ancient world, and even occasional Greco-Roman moralists, chose not to make exceptions because, loving or not, such relationships did violence to the stamp of gender impressed on the participants by nature (N34).

Powell goes on to characterize as pure "speculation" the view that Paul "would have favored excommunicating Christians who engage in homosexual activities *just as* he did believers who were involved in incestuous relationships (1 Cor. 5:1-5)" (p. 31, emphasis mine; N35). Yet that Paul would have recommended the same kind of discipline for a serial unrepentant participant in male-male intercourse as for a serial unrepentant participant in incestuous intercourse is evident from the context. The vice list in 1 Corinthians 6:9-10 is the same as the vice lists in 5:10-11, with three additional vices that merely expand on the meaning of sexually immoral people (not only participants in incest and prostitution but also adulterers and passive and active partners in male-male intercourse) and one additional vice regarding economic exploitation (not only robbers but also thieves). Repetitive, self-affirming participants in the vices of 6:9-10 risk exclusion from the kingdom of God, Paul says: "Or do you not know that unrighteous people will not inherit the kingdom of God? Stop deceiving yourselves. Neither the sexually immoral, . . . nor adulterers, nor the effeminate males who play the sexual role of females (the 'soft'), nor men who lie with males . . . shall inherit the kingdom of God." It is this view that motivated Paul to recommend a suspension or temporary ban from participation in the life of the church to persons engaged in serial unrepentant incest and in the other vices mentioned in 5:10-11 and, by inference, 6:9-10: "do not associate with anyone who calls himself a 'brother' if he is a sexually immoral person. . . . Is it not those inside [the church] that you are to judge?" (5:11-12).

The seriousness of averting exclusion from the kingdom of God demanded, once other options had been exhausted, vigorous ecclesiastical efforts at reform — up to and including removal of grave offenders from the life of the community until repentance was manifested. It obviously mattered not to Paul whether a person was a constitutional adulterer or sex addict. He believed that all Christians had the power, through the Spirit, not to be subject to the control and dominion of the sinful sexual passions of the flesh. This meant not that they would be immune from any further sinning, much less free from all temptation, but that they would at least be penitent upon the commission of sin and, in the main, regulated by the Spirit in their behavior.

Powell ends his argument on p. 31 by asserting:

> In any case, no projection of what Paul "might have thought" [N36] about this situation can be determinative for the Church's deliberations. Canonical authority extends only to what is actually written in documents that the Church confesses to be Scripture, not to what thoughts the authors of those documents might have entertained but did not record.

Well, yes and no. It depends what one means by "actually written." We have no meaningful doubt about what Paul would have thought as regards lots of situations that did not come up in the churches to which Paul writes. We let these unwritten, but utterly obvious, logical corollaries and conclusions function as though they were written. Thereby, they become "determinative for the Church's deliberations" and conveyors of "canonical authority." Perhaps I am wrong in saying this, but I should go so far as to suggest that, in practice, Powell himself tacitly operates with a similar understanding when he makes available his summary of what the Bible teaches for the ELCA's deliberations (N37).

All the same, let us turn to two examples not drawn from Powell's paper to make the point. Neither Jesus nor Paul (nor, for that matter, any NT author) said anything about bestiality. Only a handful of Old Testament texts proscribe it (Exodus 22:19; Leviticus 18:23; 20:15-16; Deuteronomy 27:21). What would Jesus and Paul have thought/done had they encountered a disciple/believer who was having regular sex with sheep? Or, turning to a specific case of incest different from the one dealt with in 1 Corinthians 5 (N38), what would Jesus or Paul have thought about a Christian man having sex with his sister? We would not say: We do not know for certain and, in any case, no projection of what they might have thought is determinative for church deliberations or carries any canonical authority. Rather, we would say that, despite the fact that those particular cases do not come up for discussion in the New Testament, it is obvious from matters of historical and literary context what Jesus and all New Testament authors would have thought, at least in general terms. They would have uttered a strong "No" to such behavior, regardless of whatever strong desires and loving intent were motivating the action in question. Would such an unwritten, but obvious, "projection" be determinative for church deliberations? Yes, in the sense that, in wrestling with whether these Levitical prohibitions carry over into the new covenant, we would conclude that the "silence" of the New Testament intimates canonical certitude across the Testaments, not canonical ambivalence (N39).

There is no great mystery about what Paul "might have thought" and "would have done" if the Corinthian believers had written back that some believing members of their community continued "to have homosexual impulses or to engage in homosexual activity that is neither promiscuous nor exploitative" (p. 31). He would have said: do not succumb to such desires; but if ever or whenever you do succumb, repent: turn back to God, experience forgiveness, and commit yourself anew to walking by the Spirit. As we have shown, Paul believed that it was an expected part of that Christian life that various sinful passions of the flesh would continue to challenge the new-creation work of the Spirit. Such passions were to be resisted if one hoped to inherit the kingdom of God. The fact of ongoing homoerotic impulses, even of an exclusive sort, would not have altered what Paul, other authors of New Testament scripture, and Jesus would have found wrong about same-sex intercourse: its same-sexness. So why should it have changed their evaluation? They understood such sexual intercourse to be a violation of the embodied complementarity of male-female unions ordained by God at creation, as told in Genesis 1-2, and embedded in nature, as evident in basic male-female differences. By attempting to join two discordant sexual halves, same-sex intercourse defiles the distinctive sexual integrity of the participants. Scripture treats this not as a relatively benign act but as a serious transgression of God's creation of gendered beings, as bad as, or worse than, incest. The difficulty of the struggle against homoerotic urges, while affecting the degree of pastoral intervention, is quite beside the point so far as assessing the behavior as a severe sin is concerned. The fact that some Christians have an exclusive pedophilic orientation in no way affects a negative evaluation of pedophilia, even when the children involved turn out asymptomatic for negative side-effects. Christians have been redeemed or bought with a price, Christ's death, not to do what they want but precisely for the purpose of glorifying God with their bodily members and eschewing all sexual immorality (1 Corinthians 6:15-20).

In short, it is indeed "determinative for the Church's deliberations" to discern what Jesus, Paul, and New Testament authors generally "might (would) have thought" about believers satisfying persistent homoerotic impulses. What they would have prescribed for the homosexual Christian involved in a committed homosexual union is apparent.

The five points made in this section, plus the preceding discussion of Genesis 1-2, demonstrate that from the perspective of Scripture same-sex intercourse is not only an intrinsically unnatural act but also an intrinsically sinful act (N40).

VI. Why the sexual orientation argument doesn't work

The Bible's alleged unawareness of something akin to a homosexual orientation is a critical assumption in Powell's discussion of exceptions. It simply had not occurred to Paul and other biblical authors — so the argument goes — that some persons, including believers, might have a persistent and dominant sexual attraction for persons of the same sex. The church has to forge a new path, based on new knowledge about sexual orientations. It is fair to say that the "orientation argument" is the dominant reason given today by prohomosex apologists for disregarding the views of Scripture on same-sex intercourse (N41). As I see it, there are three main considerations that subvert this "conventional wisdom" in prohomosex circles:

A. There were many theories in the Greco-Roman world positing biological influence on the development of one or more forms of homoerotic behavior.
B. Nothing in the language of Romans 1:24-27 suggests or depends on the view that "homosexuality" is a chosen condition of constitutional heterosexuals. In fact, the language fits quite well with a view of homoerotic passions as preexisting, controlling, and exclusive.
C. That a "homosexual orientation" would not have altered Paul's indictment of homosexual behavior is evident also from the ancient recognition of a distinction between innate predispositions and something that is "natural," as well as Paul's own view of what sin is.

It now remains to provide the documentation for these points.

A. Ancient theories of a biological basis for some homoerotic attraction

In the Greco-Roman world a number of theories existed — Platonic, Aristotelian, Hippocratic, and astrological — suggesting that at least some forms of homoerotic desire arose in part or whole from biological conditions (N42).

1. The myth of human origins expounded by Aristophanes in Plato's *Symposium* (189c-193d) traces same-sex passions to the primordial past before male-male, female-female, and male-female humans were split apart by Zeus. After the splitting, people forever longed for their other half, whether a same-sex or opposite-sex partner. "And these are they who continue with one another throughout life.... [each] desiring to join together and to be fused into a single entity with his beloved and to become one person from two" (N43).

2. Aristotelian thought speculated that some males who desired to be penetrated were so disposed "by nature"; that is, because of sperm ducts leading to the anus, thereby building pressure that requires release through the friction of penetration. Others were so disposed "from habit"; that is, owing to pleasurable childhood memories of receptive sex with an adult male and to the reinforcement of repetition. This habit "becomes like (i.e., takes on the characteristics of) nature." Habit itself was more likely to take hold "in the case of one who is both lustful and

soft (*malakos*)" — in modern-day parlance, where a person has a bio-logical predisposition toward gender nonconformity. In instances where sperm ducts led to both the anus and the penis males would desire both to penetrate and to be penetrated. "So for all those for whom na-ture is the cause, no one would describe these persons as lacking in self-control, any more than they would women because they do not take the active sexual role but the passive." Yet even "the effeminate by nature (*hoi phusei thçludriai*) . . . are constituted contrary to nature (*para phusin*)," a mistake or "defect" in nature (Aristotle, *Nicomachean Ethics* 1148b; Pseudo-Aristotle, *Problems* 4:26 [879b-880a]; N44).

3. The Hippocratic treatise *On Regimen* (1.28-29; fourth century B.C.) attributed the degree of manliness or femininity in both men and women to the mixture of male and female sperm at conception, with the sperm of each containing both male and female elements. The ex-tent to which male-based sperm or female-based sperm dominated in-fluenced the extent to which a child would become very manly or very feminine, less manly or less feminine, a male "man-woman" (an *androgynos* in passion, not necessarily in intersexed body) or "a manly woman" (*andreia*). The degree of manliness or femininity would, in turn, influence choice for an active or passive role in sexual intercourse. Biol-ogy was not everything, though; diet, education, and habits also played a part (N45). Parmenides, a pre-Socratic philosopher, held a similar con-ception (as recounted by Soranus in Caelius Aurelianus, *Chronic Dis-eases* 4.9.134-35).

4. Not referring to congenital causation but nevertheless relevant to our discussion here is an old Cretan legend retold by the Roman poet Ovid (43 B.C.-A.D. 18). According to the tale, a mother, cognizant of her husband's intense desire for a son, hid from her husband the fact that their new child was a girl. Raised as a boy (we would say: *social-ized*), Iphis developed an erotic attraction for females. When she fell in love with Ianthe, another female, she bemoaned her "monstrous" pas-sion because she recognized it to be contrary not only to custom but also to nature and divine law. And yet she was powerless to override this desire. Her tragic circumstances were resolved only when the god-dess Isis intervened to change Iphis into a male, thereby enabling her to marry Ianthe (N46). The story nicely illustrates two points: (a) social-ization can create a powerful, even irresistible, drive for a homoerotic relationship (in modern terms, nurture becoming nature); and (b) even irresistible drives can be described as contrary to nature and monstrous.

5. Soranus, an early second-century A.D. physician in Rome, wrote about chronic diseases, including why some men avidly desired pen-

etration in adulthood. The Greek text of his work no longer survives but a Latin "translation" by the fifth-century writer Caelius Aurelianus does. The part that interests us here is *On Chronic Diseases* 4.9.131-137 (N47). According to Soranus, "Many leaders of the medical schools of thought say that the disease is inherited and therefore comes down to posterity with the seed — not indeed thereby condemning nature...but condemning the human race because it held on so strongly to such vices once introduced that they could not be purged by any healing." In other words, what human society pursued eventually became an inherited disease (N48). Yet even then human responsibility was not eviscerated because, like other inherited diseases such as "gout, epilepsy, madness," this disease's negative effects could be "weakened" and made "milder" if humans strove to resist it (4.9.135-36; N49).

Soranus himself did not think that a "disease of the body" led to the development of *molles* (Gk. *malthakoi*), "soft men" eager for penetration (*subacti*) — a condition that he described as one "not from nature," insofar as it "subjugated to obscene uses parts not so intended" and disregarded "the places of our body which divine providence destined for definite functions"(4.9.131; N50). Because Soranus did not believe that "bodily treatment" could "be successfully applied to drive out the disease," he classified the condition as a "disease of the mind" (*mens* or *animus*); in other words, a psychological disorder (131-33). Accordingly, a cure could be affected only through mental processes: "One must, rather, control the mind, which is afflicted by such a deep disgrace" (133). Soranus similarly diagnosed as "afflicted by a diseased mind" "women who are called *tribades* ['those who rub']" who "practice both kinds of love" and "rush to have sex with women more than with men and pursue women with an almost masculine jealousy" (132-33; N51). For all his talk of mental illness, however, Soranus did not think the condition besetting *molles* and *tribades* was easily amenable to change. Rather, it was a chronic mental "disease" influenced indirectly by biological factors and powerful enough to "afflict" for life the bodies whose energies it sapped. He compared aggressive female bisexuality, with its dominant bent for lesbian relationships, to alcohol addiction (133). He also connected an exclusive desire on the part of males to be penetrated with a lack of virile powers in the body, particularly in old age (132, 137; N52). Elsewhere Soranus attributed some "masculine" sexual behavior on the part of women to an overly large clitoris, for which he recommends surgical removal (N53).

6. Various Greco-Roman astrologers linked up homoerotic desire with the constellation of the stars at the time of one's birth (N54). For example:

(a) According to Dositheos of Sidon (fl. A.D. 25-75), a particular lining up of Venus and the Moon can cause the birth of females "desirous of women" and males "desirous of males" of any age. Other configurations of planets can cause males to be feminized and want to have done to them "what one does in women"; or can cause females to be masculinized, doing "in women the act of men," an "unnatural" and "licentious" act (*Carmen Astrologicum* 2.7.6-17; *cf.* 2.4.21; 2.6.15; 2.26.15).

(b) Ptolemy (second century A.D.) made similar statements, adding that when Venus and Mars together appeared in masculine signs of the zodiac the conjunction could cause females not only to assume an active (masculine) sexual role with women but also to do so openly, referring to their mates as "lawful wives." Ptolemy characterized both females who played the sexual role of males and males who played the sexual role of females as having a lifelong, and apparently incurable, disease of the nonrational part of the soul (*Tetrabiblos* 3.14 §171-72; N55).

(c) Firmacus Maternus (early fourth century A.D.) also shared the same views as Dositheos, stating that particular planetary conjunctions produce males who will "always be lovers of boys" and "never wish for intercourse with women," whiles others produce those "captured by an inverted passionate desire of lust contrary to nature" (referring solely to receptive male partners?). Still others produce "mannish women" who "never couple sexually with men" and "desire intercourse with women like men," "impurely and unchastely" (N56).

Ancient astrological theories obviously have significant differences from some modern theories of innate causation. The main point, though, is that the former regard types of homoerotic attraction as congenital, lifelong, and sometimes exclusive (N57). Moreover, noteworthy is the fact that, even though these conditions are brought about by planetary configurations, the astrologers still treat at least some of these conditions as "contrary to nature" — that is, as congenital byproducts of inauspicious planetary alignments.

Thus, in the Greco-Roman milieu there was a range of theories about the development of at least some forms of homoerotic behavior that ran the gamut from, in today's terms, essentialism to social constructionism:

- A creation splitting of male-male or female-female binary humans.
- Sperm ducts leading to the anus.
- A particular mix of male and female "sperm" elements at conception.
- An inherited disease analogous to a mutated gene.
- A chronic disease of the mind or soul influenced indirectly by bio]

A disease of the soul produced by socialization factors and difficult to resist.
- The particular alignment of heavenly constellations at birth.

Particularly interesting is the close interrelationship between biology and socialization, nature and nurture, presented in a number of theories — not unlike modern scientific theory. To be sure, some of these theories are closer to contemporary speculations about homosexual causation than others. Another difference is that most of them focus more on passive receptive roles for males and active (sometimes penetrative) roles for women than on orientation *per se*. Nevertheless, the relevance of these theories cannot be discounted. First, these roles were commonly expressed in homoerotic activity, in some instances exclusively so. Second, a couple of the theories do suggest a primary homosexual orientation for some or all active males and passive females as well. Greek and Roman literature also makes references to exclusive same-sex attraction on the part of some males, even among the married. For example, the figure of Aristophanes in Plato's *Symposium* underscores that marriage for those homoerotically-oriented was a façade: "And when they reach manhood, they become lovers of boys and are not inclined *by nature* toward marriage and the procreation of children, yet are compelled to do so by the law/custom (*nomos*)" (192A-B). Third, the distinction between roles and orientation would carry less significance in a Judeo-Christian framework that held *all* homoerotic activity to be contrary to nature, not just homoerotic behavior practiced by women and feminized passive males. Differences with contemporary theories are inconsequential to the overall point: Many in the ancient world believed some homoerotic practice could be traced to interplay between biology and nurture; moreover, that homoerotic impulses could be very resistant to change. In view of the above information, it is evident that we can no longer assume that Paul was incapable of conceiving of some biological causation for at least some forms of homoerotic proclivity and behavior (for a detailed comparison with Philo's views, see N58).

Indeed, it is inconceivable that Paul would have been totally unaware of boys in the Greco-Roman world who, from their earliest period of sexual awareness, were socialized as the receptive partners of insertive males and who, as adults, continued to desire — in many instances exclusively so — sex with other adult males. Philo was aware of them and he speaks of their being "accustomed" and "accustoming themselves" at an early age to desiring such practices as part of their transformation into females, which worked in their very souls a disease "hard to fight against" (*Abraham* 136; *Contemplative Life* 60; *Special Laws* 3.37). Paul's reference to the *malakoi* ("soft men") in 1 Corinthians 6:9 cinches the assumption that he knew of the existence of lifelong homoerotic proclivity.

B. The wording of Romans 1:24-27

Given the number and range of theories for homoerotic attraction circulating in the Greco-Roman world, it is likely that Paul was aware of the possibility that some persons were disposed, through a combination of biological and social factors, to sex with persons of the same sex, sometimes exclusively so. Certainly there is nothing in the wording of Romans 1:24-27 that suggests that "homosexuality" is a *chosen* condition of constitutional heterosexuals. Obviously consensual behavior is always, by definition, chosen. But the relationship between choice and the biologically related impulses that stimulate behavior is more complex. Romans 1:24-27 reflects this fact.

1. *On the link to idolatry.* Romans 1:18-32 does not picture idolatry (in the literal sense of worshipping statues) as a necessary prerequisite for homoerotic passion any more than it does for any other form of "sexual uncleanness" (*akatharsia*, 1:24) or for covetousness and envy (1:29). The text refers to collective entities, not individuals, and to widespread effect, not origin (for the origin of sin, see 5:12-21). The possibility of non-idolatrous believers engaging in "sexual uncleanness," including same-sex intercourse, was a prospect that Paul vigorously warned against (Romans 6:19-22; 1 Corinthians 6:9-11; N59).

2. *On "exchanging" and "leaving behind" natural intercourse with the opposite sex.* The references in Romans 1:26-27 to the fact that "females *exchanged* (*metellaxan*) the natural use for what was contrary to nature" and to "the males *leaving behind* (*aphentes*) the natural use of the female" do *not* describe a choice of homosexual *desire* over heterosexual desire (as is commonly assumed by pro-homosex scholars). Rather, they describe a choice of *behavior* stimulated by disoriented passions over behavior motivated by nature. *Nature* here refers to the clear revelation of male-female complementarity in material creation. Humans deliberately suppressed this clear revelation in order to satisfy cravings for same-sex intercourse (N60). Paul's point parallels his observation about the exchange of God for idols (1:18-23). The exchange is one of reality for unreality, a clear revelation known in the material world of creation and nature for the foolish imaginations of a darkened heart and unfit mind (N61). Nothing in the wording assumes an experience of heterosexual desire or behavior prior to engaging in homosexual sex. Also,

the words "exchanged" and "leaving behind" suggest exclusive homo-erotic behavior rather than a bisexual life.

3. *On "giving over" and "desire."* The very language of "God gave them over" (*paredoken autous ho theos*) in 1:24, 26, 28 presupposes preexisting sinful desires beyond human control. Otherwise, to what did God hand them over? The idea of dominant sinful sexual desires is precisely the picture presented later in Romans 6:15-23 when Paul speaks of the pre-Christian life of his audience of Roman believers. Formerly they lacked the very freedom to do right, enslaved as they were to "sexual uncleanness" and to other forms of "lawless behavior" (6:19) and with-out the counterbalancing power of the Spirit (7:6). Paul does not claim that these desires are eradicated in the Christian life (Galatians 5:17). They are instead brought under the management of the Spirit. *Desire* (*epithumia*, 1:24) is picked up again in Romans 7:7-23 as an innate im-pulse in the human body beyond ultimate human control.

4. *On being "inflamed" with passion.* The language of being "inflamed with their yearning for one another, males with males" (1:27) also sug-gests homoerotic desires that are both exclusive and controlling. It is sometimes claimed that Paul's main concern in Romans 1:24-27 was with excess passion, not with same-sex intercourse per se; or that Paul's remarks can be disregarded because we now know that homosexual orientations do not stem from excessive lust (N62). However, in antiq-uity "excess passion" never constituted an independent critique of same-sex intercourse. Passion was judged as excessive (e.g., the passion for sex with animals) on the basis of other criteria about behavioral limits. Otherwise, how could one determine which passions were in excess? There has to be some prior determination that something is wrong with the behavior in question in order to characterize it as excess passion. Paul likely viewed any shocking transgression of God-ordained bound-aries to be — by definition — an overheating or excess of desire, in the sense of desiring something that God did not ordain humans to desire by virtue of creation intent and design.

C. Why a "homosexual orientation" would not have mattered

Given the pervasive, strong, and absolute opposition of Scripture gen-erally, and Paul particularly, to same-sex intercourse, the burden of proof ought to rest on those who contend that cognizance of sexual orienta-tions would have made a difference to Paul's views. As it is, the evi-dence indicates that such alleged "new knowledge" would not have made any significant difference to Paul's assessment of homosexual intercourse — even if it could be established (and it cannot) that Paul did not have the slightest inkling about the biologically related, exclusive character of some forms of same-sex attraction.

1. *What precisely is this "new knowledge"?* Modern socio-scientific evidence has *not* demonstrated that homoerotic "orientations" arise directly and primarily from congenital factors, whether genes, intrauterine hormonal influences, or special homosexual brains. Evidence to date suggests that congenital influence is largely indirect and subordinate to socialization factors, both microcultural (family and peer) and macrocultural (conventions, instructions, and sanctions). Limitations of space imposed on this essay do not permit the laying out of evidence; for that I refer the reader to other materials (N63). Here I simply quote briefly from three separate studies that I mention in my book:

(a) From J. Michael Bailey's latest identical twin study, which minimizes the sample bias of earlier twin studies, including his own: "In contrast to most prior twin studies of sexual orientation...ours did not provide statistically significant support for the importance of genetic factors" (N64).

(b) From David Greenberg's cross-cultural study of homosexuality: "Where social definitions of appropriate and inappropriate behavior are clear and consistent, with positive sanctions for conformity and negative ones for nonconformity, virtually everyone will conform irrespective of genetic inheritance and, to a considerable extent, irrespective of personal psychodynamics" (N65).

(c) From the 1992 National Health and Social Life Survey (NHSLS, Laumann et al.), conducted mainly by University of Chicago researchers and commenting on the disparity in homosexual self-identification as one moves from rural to urban environments: "An environment that provides increased opportunities for and fewer negative sanctions against same-gender sexuality may both allow and even elicit expression of same-gender interest and sexual behavior" (N66).

No one is predestined from the womb to become homosexual. Parents, peers, societal expectations and sanctions, and a person's own incremental choices play the major role in determining whether homosexuality will develop for any given individual. The point to be made here is that biblical scholars, uninformed about both Greco-Roman theories of congenital causation and modern socio-scientific work, tend to exaggerate the distance between ancient and modern views. It turns out that the ancients were not so ignorant about sexual orientations, while we are not so informed about homosexual orientation as impervious to cultural manipulation. Suddenly the "new knowledge" does not look quite so new, with the result that claims of it justifying a radical shift in biblical interpretation carry much less weight.

2. *Calling some innate homoerotic desire "contrary to nature" in the ancient world.* Even some of the Greco-Roman texts theorizing biological influence designated the activity as contrary to nature. This was particularly the case with males who desired to be penetrated (*cf.* the Aristotelian texts, the medical text by Soranus, and the astrological texts). The ancients observed that not everything given *by nature* is constituted *according to nature* (*cf.* Aristotle, *Nicomachean Ethics* 1148b). Persons' desires can be at odds with their essential sex. We still recognize the validity of such a distinction. Nature makes mistakes that are not in accord with its well-working processes; for example, severe congenital defects, disease, a predisposition toward alcoholism, and biologically related sexual attractions to children. Now, if these "pagan" texts could make such a distinction within a cultural milieu that did not indict severely *all* participants in homoerotic behavior, what is the likelihood that Paul would have stopped calling same-sex intercourse "contrary to nature" had he only known of a homosexual orientation? The idea is inconceivable, given that Paul operated within a scriptural and cultural milieu that regarded all same-sex intercourse as contrary to God's creation design. Does anyone want to argue that Paul would have ended up *more* open to homosexual activity than his Greek and Roman counterparts when in fact he started with a more unequivocal view?

3. *Nature for Paul as something structurally broader than "sexual orientation."* Paul too did not characterize all biologically related impulses as existing *according to nature.* He distinguished between, on the one hand, innate passions perverted by the fall and exacerbated by idol worship and, on the other hand, that part of material creation least likely to be marred by human sin. The latter would be the best indication of God's intended structural design for human sexuality. Immediately following his reference to same-sex intercourse is a list of other vices that certainly have some innate basis — for example, covetousness, envy, and arrogance — and yet do not for that reason accord with nature (Rom1:29-31). Innate desires are notoriously unreliable indicators of God's will, as an array of sexually impure impulses also proves. By *nature* Paul meant God's intended design for creation, still visible and evident in material structures despite the introduction of sin into the world. Paul would never have described as *according to nature* a sexual orientation that, from a scriptural standpoint, was incompatible with essential embodied existence as a gendered being. There are two sexes, each structurally configured and open-ended to the other. Neither male sexuality nor female sexuality represents, by itself, whole sexuality. If a sexual merger with another is to be had, it must be with "the other half"

in order to become a sexually whole, "one flesh" being. The absence of a gender complement in same-sex intercourse and the attendant violation of the stamp of gender on the sexual self — the *malakoi* in 1 Corinthians 6:9 are an extreme case in point — are nature's primary clues.

4. *The compatibility of Paul's view of sin.* Even exaggerated claims about what we now know regarding homosexual orientation are essentially compatible with Paul's own view of sin. In Romans 5 and 7 Paul speaks of sin as:

    a. An innate impulse
    b. Operating in the human body
    c. Transmitted by an ancestor human
    d. Never entirely within human control

In Paul's understanding these elements do not disqualify an impulse from being sinful; they rather define sin as sin. Why then would the notion of biological causation for some homoerotic attraction have made any difference to Paul's view of same-sex intercourse? If Paul could be transported into the twenty-first century and told that homoerotic desires have (at most) a partial and indirect connection to innate causation factors, he doubtless would have said either "I could have told you that" or at very least "That fits well into my own understanding of sin."

5. *Applying the orientation argument to other sins.* The mere fact of an entrenched impulse not being consciously chosen by some is not grounds for its acceptance.

- Some alcoholism, criminal behavior, and a whole range of non-criminal vices (e.g., selfishness, jealousy, greed, lust) can be described along these lines.

- While some people are quite content with a single sex partner for life, large numbers of men and some women find it extraordinarily difficult to limit their number of life-time sex-partners to one, or even a dozen. Have they chosen this condition?

- Indirect congenital factors and early childhood experiences can significantly affect a person's potential for entering into a committed, lifelong sexual union. We do not enter marriage on a level playing field.

- Most of us grow up with an aversion to having sex with close blood relations. "The common childish phrase that something is as unappealing as 'kissing your own sister' reflects a real, cross-cultural, psychological phenomenon" (N67). Yet some do not have such an "instinctive" aversion. Did they choose not to have it?

- Dr. Fred Berlin, founder of the Sexual Disorders Clinic at Johns Hopkins and leading specialist on pedophilia, said in a recent interview (*People Magazine*, 4/15/02) that:

  Sexual abuse during childhood is not the cause, but it is a risk factor. . . . The biggest misconception about pedophilia is that someone chooses to have it. . . . It's not anyone's fault that they have it, but it's their responsibility to do something about it. . . . Biological factors play into [the development of pedophilia]. . . . We've learned that you can successfully treat people with pedophilia, but you cannot cure them.

The bottom line is that discerning the morality of a given disposition has little to do with whether it is "fixed early in life." The latter should affect the degree of pastoral sensitivity but not whether the behavior should be condoned.

If it were otherwise, then consistency and logic would compel a radical departure from Christian ethics, at least as enunciated by Jesus and the early apostolic church. Henceforth, the ultimate consideration for determining the morality of a given behavior would be the degree to which the behavior emanated from an entrenched impulse, via congenital influences and/or early childhood socialization. So long as one could not prove, in advance and in scientifically measurable ways, inevitable and enduring harm — for this is the standard that pro-homosex advocates impose on "pro-comp" advocates — the actor's "orientation," of whatever kind, would define the morality of the act. Certainly from a Pauline perspective sin would cease to be sin. Commandments, whether from the teachings of Jesus or some other part of Scripture, would cease to be commandments in any meaningful sense. Humans would be little more than the sum total of their fleshly impulses, the measure of their own selves. What remaining significance the indwelling Spirit would have — if not to override fleshly impulses, crucify the self, and enable obedience in behavior to God's commands — I know not. Jesus Christ himself would be dethroned from the status of Lord. In his place constitutional predisposition would reign. The rightness or wrongness of various types of hitherto immoral sexual practices would depend largely on the particular sexual libidos of the actors, rather than on a God-given standard to which human sexual libidos are subjected. These are the implications just for sexual relations. Extend the same principles to other areas of ethics and the church is left with complete and utter moral chaos.

By now the conclusion should be clear: There is little to commend the "orientation argument" as a means of extracting exceptions to Scripture's prohibition of homosexual practice. The evidence does not support the assumption that Paul could not have conceived of a relatively entrenched and exclusive form of homoeroticism — much less that knowledge of such would have caused Paul and all the other writers of Scripture to do a complete about-face on homosexual practice. The issue of structural complementarity — male and female as the respective halves to a sexual whole — is not materially affected by the presence or absence of a "homosexual orientation."

VII. Concluding Observations

I have made three main points in this essay:

1. Understood both within their historical context and in later interpretation by Jesus and Paul, the Genesis creation stories view sexual intercourse as something more than an activity designed for pleasure or for establishing durable bonds of intimacy. Sexual intercourse is about remerging with another into a single sexual whole. Accordingly, these stories regard the presence of complementary sexual others, male and female, as an absolutely essential *prerequisite* for acceptable sexual intercourse. Homosexual relations are a necessarily sinful, extreme affront to this vision of normative sexual unions. While the creation stories may treat being in a sexual relationship with a person of the other sex as merely "the normal state of affairs," they view the other-sex status of one's sexual partner as nonnegotiable. Genesis 2:18, "it is not good for the human to be alone," cannot be wrenched from its context and used to pry exceptions from this prescriptive biblical norm. At most Genesis 2:18 offers a *conditional* opportunity for sexual intimacy. The prerequisites for acceptable sexual intercourse, including an other-sex partner, must first be met.

2. That the Bible regards same-sex intercourse as *intrinsically* sinful, and not just normally or mildly so, is further confirmed by a discussion of the Levitical prohibitions, the nature argument in Romans 1:26-27, the terms *malakoi* and *arsenokoitai* (1 Corinthians 6:9) in their literary context, and Paul's recognition that some of his converts might experience an intense ongoing struggle with homoerotic impulses.

3. The notion that modern awareness of "homosexual orientation" challenges Scripture's absolute prohibition of homosexual intercourse simply does not square with the evidence. It does not do justice to ancient theories of a biological basis for some homoerotic attraction, to the

wording of Paul's critique of same-sex intercourse in Romans 1:24-27, or to Paul's view of sin generally. In particular, it ignores the fact that in the ancient context, not to mention our own, even innate homoerotic impulses could be categorized as "contrary to nature" and sinful.

Persons in the church today who espouse a view of "exceptions" to a normative biblical prohibition of same-sex intercourse often locate themselves, as Mark Powell does, in the middle of a spectrum of "biblically consistent views," between the twin "extremes" of an absolute prohibition of same-sex intercourse and a complete annulment of the Bible's prohibition (pp. 38-39). Such posturing is self-deceiving. The evidence is overwhelming that *any* approval of homosexual behavior represents a "biblically *in*consistent view," whether it is a matter of "exceptional" cases involving thousands or an embrace of every committed homosexual union. Far from occupying a putative middle, the "exceptions view" is not even at an end of a spectrum of biblically consistent views. It lies outside the spectrum. Maintaining Scripture's one and only absolute stance against all same-sex intercourse is no more extreme than maintaining an absolute stance against incest, adultery, plural marriages, pedophilia, sex with prostitutes, or bestiality — sexual behaviors that involve structural incongruities. One does not occupy the middle by making exceptions. One occupies the middle by loving those who commit sexual offenses and showing a readiness to restore the penitent without reprisal, while firmly rejecting the sinful behavior and expressing concern for the offender's inheritance of God's kingdom.

One also often hears from the prohomosex side: "Discussions of *application* of Scripture. . . . are matters on which good and faithful Christians will disagree" (so Powell, pp. 33-34; *cf.* the book's title: *Faithful Conversation*). *As applied to the issue of homosexual practice*, the statement is premature, preemptive, and presumptuous. Yes, good and faithful Christians have leeway to disagree about various important, yet nonessential, applications of Scripture (e.g., as regards mainline denominational differences over baptism and the Eucharist). But no, not every disagreement about the application of Scripture can be described as a dispute within the circle of "good and faithful Christians." Some applications can be grossly unfaithful, despite the best intentions of the interpreters, and can lead to catastrophic results for the community of faith.

Again, the example of incest in 1 Corinthians 5 is a case in point. In other respects, the Corinthian believers may have been faithful (*cf.* 11:2). Yet in this particular issue they had seriously departed from the faith. The incestuous man's erroneous application of the gospel had led him to commit behavior that endangered his salvation. Given Paul's vigorous response, there can be little doubt that, had the Corinthians not withdrawn their support for his behavior, they would have severed themselves from communities of faith elsewhere and exposed themselves to the fearful judgment of God.

This is precisely the situation that the ELCA and other mainline denominations now find themselves in as they contemplate departing from Scripture's unequivocal witness against homosexual practice. Remaining faithful to the core value that God intends sexually intimate relationships for, and only for, the remerging of complementary sexual others into a sexual whole is a gravely serious matter on which the fate of the church and many individuals rest. This belief is a foundational starting point for all sexual ethics. It is assuredly not a matter of indifference over which faithful Christians can agree to disagree. May the church not deceive itself into thinking otherwise.

Robert A. J. Gagnon is Associate Professor of New Testament at Pittsburgh Theological Seminary. He is the author of The Bible and Homosexual Practice: Texts and Hermeneutics *(Abingdon Press, 2001; 520 pp.) and co-author of* Homosexuality and the Bible: Two Views *(Fortress Press, 2003). He has also published a number of articles in scholarly journals, including* Journal of Biblical Literature, New Testament Studies, Novum Testamentum, *and* Catholic Biblical Quarterly. *Dr. Gagnon is a frequent guest speaker in Lutheran, Presbyterian, Episcopalian, and Methodist gatherings.*

---

[1] At approximately 42,000 words, my original essay was too long to be incorporated in its entirety into this volume. Accordingly, I have placed sections I-III of the original, plus the notes for sections IV-VI, on my website at http://www.robgagnon.net. For the convenience of readers of this essay I give short summaries below of sections I-III. For sections IV-VI, I have inserted note numbers at the appropriate points in this essay, corresponding to note numbers in the online copy (e.g., "N1" designating note 1 online). Readers do not need to consult the online material in order to make sense of this essay, though the online material will provide further elucidation of various points. Readers who do not have access to the Internet and would like to make arrangements for securing a paper copy of the online material can contact the author at Pittsburgh Theological Seminary, 616 N. Highland Ave., Pittsburgh, PA 15206-2596.

[2] http://www.robgagnon.net

[3] In order of degree of engagement with the specifics of Powell's argument, from least to the greatest, readers will encounter:

• *Section VI. Why the Sexual Orientation Argument Does Not Work.* This section treats Powell's arguments only marginally, for two reasons: (1) Powell does not have much new to say about the orientation issue; and (2) nearly all of section VI was originally written with my recent Fortress Press essay in mind. The discussion in section VI is essential for assessing the correctness of Powell's position. But it is of equal relevance for any prohomosex argument that touts "homosexual orientation" as a significant reason for overturning the Bible's witness against same-sex intercourse.

• *Section IV. The Male-Female Prerequisite in the Genesis Creation Stories.* Only the last subsection of section IV ("F. Implications for Powell's view") specifically deals with Powell's arguments regarding Genesis 2:18-24. Since Powell makes the strongest case — relatively speaking — for a (partly) prohomosex reading of this text, it is fitting that I focus the final subsection on his work.

• *Section V. The Rest of the Case For Regarding Same-Sex Intercourse as Intrinsically Sinful.* This section is heavily engaged with the main exegetic.al argument of Powell's essay because Powell is the strongest advocate — again, relatively speaking — for the view that the Bible's stance on same-sex intercourse, while normative, does not preclude the possibility of exceptions. Yet even this section can stand alone as a coherent argument against any prohomosex attempt to restrict the biblical prohibition to certain kinds of homosexual practice.

[4] http://www.robgagnon.net

[5] Ibid.

[6] Ibid.

Chapter Nine

Homosexuality in Ecumenical Perspective

By Jay Scott Newman, J.C.L.

I accepted the invitation to submit this essay most enthusiastically because I come to all matters ecumenical rather naturally. You see, I was born to a family of Baptists and Brethren. I became an atheist at age thirteen. I was brought to Jesus Christ at age nineteen by God-fearing, Calvin-quoting Presbyterians. I was born again by water and the Holy Spirit in an Anglican font; my sponsors in Baptism were a Methodist man and a Lutheran woman. At age twenty I was received into full communion with the Catholic Church. In short, I have been almost everything except a Buddhist, and last March, after the second child-molesting Catholic bishop of Palm Beach resigned in disgrace, I very briefly considered following the Excellent Eightfold Path.

In truth, my own personal story illustrates a point central to my theme today: All discipleship begins with conversion. "The time is fulfilled, and the Kingdom of God is at hand; repent, and believe in the gospel" (Mark: 1:15).

What we seek in ecumenism

Repent, and believe in the gospel. Let us bear in mind these solemn words of the Lord Jesus as we consider the ecumenical implications of proposals in the ELCA and other Protestant communions to change the settled and received Christian teaching on marriage, ministry, homosexual behavior, and the authority and truth of Scripture.

To understand the ecumenical consequences of these proposals, it is first necessary to know what the Catholic Church seeks in ecumenism.

Pope John Paul II spoke to this point in his 1995 encyclical letter, *Ut Unum Sint*. "The ultimate goal of the ecumenical movement," the Pope wrote, "is to reestablish full, visible unity among all the baptized" (*Ut Unum Sint*, 77).

So, the goal of ecumenism is not merely comity, it is unity — full, visible unity. We are striving not simply to be nice to each other but to be in full communion with each other. And this is in obedience to the High Priestly Prayer of the Lord Jesus offered in the night before his death (*cf.* John 17:20-26). To seek anything other than full, visible communion among all the baptized is to settle for less than Christ wills for his church.

But where is this unity to be found? Again, Pope John Paul: "The unity willed by God can be attained only by the adherence of all to the content of revealed faith in its entirety. In matters of faith, compromise is in contradiction with God, who is truth. In the Body of Christ, the way, the truth, and the life, who could consider legitimate a reconciliation brought about at the expense of truth?" (*Ut Unum Sint*, 18). So, to find unity we must accept the truth of revelation in the obedience of faith. And the obstacle to such acceptance is sin. "If we say we have no sin, we deceive ourselves, and the truth is not in us" (1 John 1:8). For this reason, the Second Vatican Council connects ecumenism to conversion — personal conversion and communal conversion. "If you continue in my word, you are truly my disciples, and you will know the truth, and the truth will make you free" (John 8:31-32). John Paul explains that love for the truth is the deepest dimension of any authentic quest for full communion among Christians. As the Second Vatican Council insists, there is no genuine love for the truth apart from the obedience of faith by which man fully commits his entire self to God, offering the complete submission of intellect and will to God who reveals, and freely and completely assenting to the truth revealed by God (*cf. Dei Verbum*, 5).

Of course, to make this act of faith is a work of grace, and the interior action of the Holy Spirit must precede and assist the free act of submission of the intellect and will, moving the heart and turning it to God, opening the eyes of the mind and giving the believer the grace of assenting to the truth promptly, joyfully, and easily. But apart from this obedience of faith, there is no true discipleship and no genuine evangelical freedom — only the slavery of sin and error. True evangelical freedom is the liberty to do everything we should, not the license to do whatever we want. And to live in this freedom we must continue in the Word of God.

The other essayists in this volume have clearly established, I believe, that homogenital behavior is, even if unintentionally, a form of rebellion against God, and that is a tragedy for those caught in such a habit. This personal tragedy, however, will be transformed into communal chaos if the revisionists win the day. In his magisterial commentary on St. Paul's *Letter to the Romans*, Karl Barth considers verses 28 to 31 of chapter 1. Of those who surrender to homosexual lusts, Barth writes:

> ...they became no longer capable of serious awe and amazement. They became unable to reckon with anything except feelings and experience and events. They think only in terms of more or less spiritual sophistry, without light from above or from behind. Here is the final vacuity and disintegration. Chaos has found itself, and anything may happen. The atoms whirl, the struggle for existence rages. Even reason itself becomes irrational. Ideas of duty and of fellowship become wholly unstable. The world is full of personal caprice and social unrighteousness. (*The Epistle to the Romans*, p. 53).

Anyone who doubts Barth's conclusions need spend only a little while in the right districts of any of our major cities. The quiet homosexuality of dons has been set aside by the violent revolution of deconstruction. The love that dare not speak its name has become the love which will not shut up, and the whirlwind rages even in the church. The spiritual sophistry of which Barth wrote is the engine which drives revisionists and dissidents in every Christian communion, including my own. This form of sophistry is found described in Scripture in another context, in a discussion about love of neighbor. Having been taught by the Lord Jesus that he must love his neighbor, a lawyer asks in retort, "And who is my neighbor?" *In the Cost of Discipleship*, Dietrich Bonhoeffer lays bare the rebellious sophistry behind these words:

> How often has this question been asked, in good faith and genuine ignorance! It is plausible enough and any earnest seeker of the truth could reasonably ask it. But this is not the way the lawyer meant it. Jesus parries the question as a temptation of the devil, and that in fact is the whole point of the parable of the Good Samaritan. It is the sort of question you can keep on asking without ever getting an answer. Its source lies in the wrangling of men, corrupted in mind and bereft of truth; of men doting about questionings and disputes of words. From it "cometh envy, strife, railings, even surmisings." (1 Timothy 6:4ff) It is the question of men who

are puffed up, men who are "ever learning, and never able to come to knowledge of the truth." Of men "holding a form of godliness, but having denied the power thereof." (2 Timothy 3:5 ff) They cannot believe, and they keep on asking this same question because they are 'branded in their own conscience as with a hot iron,' (1 Timothy 4:2) because they refuse to obey the Word of God. Who is my neighbor? Does this question admit of any answer? Is it my kinsman, my compatriot, my brother Christian, or my enemy? There is an element of truth and falsehood in each of these answers. The whole question lands us into doubt and disobedience, and it is a veritable act of rebellion against the commandment of God (*The Cost of Discipleship*, p. 77).

Does the Bible really demand celibate chastity of those who are drawn to others of their own sex? Can't we find a way in the church for our homosexual brothers and sisters to enjoy quasi-spousal love? Would God really expect anybody to live in loneliness? Many in the churches keep on asking these and similar questions over and over because they cannot believe and they will not obey the Word of God. But, as a courageous Lutheran pastor taught us, there is no cheap grace, and the church cannot preach a gospel other than one given once and for all to the saints.

The debate now raging in the ELCA and elsewhere is usually framed by the revisionists as a choice between compassion and legalism, between understanding and fear, between tolerance and hatred. But these are not the true terms of the debate. We are, instead, confronted with a choice between the gospel and its competitors, between the Bible and the manuals of the sexual revolution. And in this contest, what are we to believe? What is the truth about homosexuality and chastity?

Allow me quote for you three very brief paragraphs on homosexuality found in the *Catechism of the Catholic Church* (CCC) and then conclude with two short paragraphs on chastity.

Homosexuality refers to relations between men or between women who experience an exclusive or predominant sexual attraction toward persons of the same sex. It has taken a great variety of forms through the centuries and in different cultures. Its psychological genesis remains largely unexplained. Basing itself on Scripture, which presents homosexual acts as acts of grave depravity (*cf.* Genesis 19:1-29, Romans 1:24-27, 1 Corinthians 6:10, 1 Timothy 1:10), tradition has always declared that "homosexual acts are intrinsically disordered" (CDF, *Persona humana* 8). They are contrary to the natural law. They close the sexual act to the gift of life. They do not proceed from a genuine affective and sexual complementarity. Under no circumstances can they be approved.

The number of men and women who have deep-seated homosexual tendencies is not negligible. This inclination, which is objectively disordered, constitutes for most of them a trial. They must be accepted with respect, compassion, and sensitivity. Every sign of unjust discrimination in their regard should be avoided. These persons are called to fulfill God's will in their lives and, if they are Christians, to unite to the sacrifice of the Lord's Cross the difficulties they may encounter from their condition. Homosexual persons are called to chastity. By the virtues of self-mastery that teach them inner freedom, at times by the support of disinterested friendship, by prayer and sacramental grace, they can and should gradually and resolutely approach Christian perfection (*CCC* 2357-2359).

Lest this call to chastity, however, seem an unfair burden imposed upon homosexuals, here is what our catechism says on the obligation of all Christians to seek this virtue:

All the baptized are called to chastity. The Christian has "put on Christ" (Galations 3:27), the model for all chastity. All Christ's faithful are called to lead a chaste life in keeping with their particular states of life. At the moment of his Baptism, the Christian is pledged to lead his affective life in chastity.

People should cultivate chastity in the way that is suited to their state of life. Some profess virginity or consecrated celibacy which enables them to give themselves to God alone with an undivided heart in a remarkable manner. Others live in the way prescribed for all by the moral law, whether they are married or single. Married people are called to live conjugal chastity; other practice chastity in continence: "There are three forms of the virtue of chastity: the first is that of spouses, the second that of widows, and the third that of virgins. We do not praise any one of them to the exclusion of the others... This is what makes for the richness of the discipline of the Church" (St. Ambrose, *De Vid uis* 4, 23: PL 16, 255A). (*CCC* 2348-2)

These brief words summarize what the Catholic Church believes and teaches (and has always believed and taught) about the disorder of homosexuality and the virtue of chastity. Please notice that explicit appeal is made to the truth and authority of Scripture. For this reason, the Catholic Church regards this teaching as divinely revealed, as preserved by the Holy Spirit from all error, as irreformable, and as necessary to believe and to live by for all who would follow Christ.

Departing from the gospel

To put the matter another way: Any Christian who believes a doctrine on homosexuality and chastity contrary to that found in Scripture is by that fact no longer in full communion with Jesus Christ and his holy church. And any communion of Christians which teaches a doctrine on homosexuality and chastity contrary to that revealed in Scripture has *to that degree* departed from the gospel and thereby *to that degree* separated itself from the Word of God and therefore from the Body of Christ.

What the consequences would be for individual Christians who found themselves in a communion formally teaching a doctrine contrary to the revealed Word of God I cannot say. But surely there would be consequences; heresy always has consequences. And the consequences for orthodox believers within a communion teaching heresy could only be dire.

I can, however, speak to the consequences of such infidelity for ecumenism: The Catholic Church could never be in full communion with any Christian body that teaches a doctrine about anything, including human sexuality, which contradicts the revealed truth of the gospel.

Now, I can well imagine that some of you are thinking: "Those are fine words, but don't the priest sex scandals in 2002 put the lie to your words?" It is a fair question, but the simple and true answer is No. In fact, understanding how and why the Catholic Church in the United States came to the sorry state it is in today illustrates precisely what happens when the truth about God is rejected for a lie.

I commend to you most highly a book just published by George Weigel called *The Courage to be Catholic: Crisis, Reform, and the Future of the Church*. Weigel makes a compelling case for the correlation between organized rejection of Catholic teaching about human sexuality and the pathological parade of sexually predatory priests and ineffectual or malfeasant bishops. Celibacy no more causes child abuse than marriage causes adultery; lack of fidelity to the gospel and to one's baptismal promises does. It is hard enough to live in keeping with the Gospel's call to chastity when we are convinced of its truth, but we soon will not even try when we are convinced that it is false. And the sad fact is that

thousands upon thousands of Catholics — many of them priests and religious, some of them bishops — do not believe and have not believed
for many long years that the church is teaching the truth about human
sexuality. Dissent, organized and principled repudiation of the Catholic Church's solemn teaching of the gospel, is raised up by the revisionists as a banner of progress and freedom, but this is the merely the slavery of rebellion first disguised as liberty by the Father of Lies in the
Garden. Sadly, many deluded souls have exchanged the revealed truth
about God and man for the idolatrous postulates of the sexual revolution and other fantasies. Given this fact, should we be surprised when a
few wretched priests prey upon boys? And let this tragedy serve as a
warning to those in the ELCA who would overturn received Christian
teaching about human sexuality in the service of the homosexual agenda.
Again, Barth: "Here is the final vacuity and disintegration. Chaos has
found itself, and anything may happen. Even reason itself becomes ir-
rational. Ideas of duty and of fellowship become wholly unstable. The
world is full of personal caprice and social unrighteousness." So, where
do we go from here? Where we always go — to Jesus Christ and him
crucified.

Contrasting wisdom

In the 19th century, John Henry Newman diagnosed the central religious struggle of his time and our time: the battle between revealed
religion and its counterfeits, the struggle between the "folly" of God's
wisdom and the "wisdom" of human folly (cf. 1 Corinthians 1:18-31).
Our brothers and sisters in the church who seek to change the settled
and received Christian teaching on chastity, homosexuality, marriage,
and ministry are not, most of them, consciously or deliberately seeking
to overthrow the gospel and replace it with a lie. But by rejecting the
authority of Scripture and by attempting to interpret divine revelation
in clear contradiction to its plain meaning, that is what they are doing.
This fight is not first and last about sex; it is about the truth of the Bible.
In defending that truth we must propose to our brothers and sisters in
Christ who are burdened with homosexual desire a more excellent way,
the way of God's love revealed in the life, death, and Resurrection of
Jesus Christ, the way of genuine discipleship, the Way of the Cross.
Any Christian communion that does less than this is unfaithful to the
Word of God and complicit in the death — spiritual and sometimes physi-
cal — of her children. The gospel is the power of God unto salvation for
all who believe; in it the righteousness of God is revealed (cf. Romans
1:16-17). The task of the church is always and everywhere to bear faith-

ful witness to the gospel and lead the whole human race to salvation through union with Christ Jesus by Word and Sacrament.

In this long struggle to preserve and present the full truth about God and man, we must rely upon God's grace to sustain us and keep us faithful. In the Roman Missal there is a "Mass for the Spread of the Gospel," and the secondary Collect of that Mass could serve as the prayer for those seeking full, visible communion among all the baptized and for those striving to refute dissent and fulfill the Great Commission in fidelity to the Word of God:

> "God our Father, you sent your Son into the world to be its true light. Pour out the Holy Spirit he promised us to sow the truth in men's hearts and awaken in them obedience to the faith. May all men be born again to the new life of baptism and enter the fellowship of your one, holy people. This we ask through Christ our Lord. Amen."

Jay Scott Newman is pastor of St. Mary's Roman Catholic Church in Greenville, South Carolina. He is a frequent lecturer in ecumenical settings and a contributor to many journals.

 Appendix

A Pastoral Statement of Conviction and Concern

Presented at the Conference on Christian Sexuality
Sponsored by the American Lutheran Publicity Bureau
(Publishers of *Lutheran Forum* and *Forum Letter*)
Ruskin Heights Lutheran Church, Kansas City, Missouri
October 24-26, 2002

The Evangelical Lutheran Church in America is in the midst of studies on human sexuality. We wish to be a part of this process and to be active participants in the conversation. We do so in reliance on the Spirit's power to keep the church faithful to its Biblical and confessional heritage. We also do so with the intention to "maintain the unity of the Spirit in the bond of peace" (Ephesians 4:3).

We offer the following statement as a way of summarizing our position on human sexuality and as our way of affirming what the church has taught and confessed on these issues since apostolic times.

1. The Bible and the Christian Tradition, including the Lutheran Confessions, see sexuality as integrally related to the doctrine of marriage. Marriage, an institution ordained by God, is the life-long union of one man and one woman for the creation of human life and for their mutual love and care. Sexual intercourse is not a fundamental private right or psychological necessity, but a gift of God. Its purpose is to serve as a means of uniting husband and wife and continuing God's life-creating work. The confessions teach that we are to "live chastely in thought, word, and deed in (our) particular situation" *(Large Catechism* 394:219, Tappert trans.). Sexual intercourse is part of the vocation of marriage and is misused in any other context.

2. The gospel frees us from the curse of the law, that is, the judgment that falls on us because we are sinners. It does not free us from the righteous life that the law summarizes. "You, having been set free from sin,

have become slaves of righteousness" (Romans 6:18). The freedom of the gospel does not make the forbidden permissible; rather, that freedom encourages and enables us to embrace joyfully a life of faithful service and holy living. In Christ we are given the grace, by the Holy Spirit, to "know how to control (our) own body in holiness and honor" (1 Thessalonians 4:4).

3. We view any change in the church's doctrine of marriage as a grave error. The Evangelical Lutheran Church in America is currently studying whether the church may bless homosexual relationships, and whether the church may ordain sexually active homosexuals to the office of the ministry. Such proposed changes in Christian doctrine distort the Biblical record, appeal to questionable scientific theories, suppress inconvenient data, and rely overwhelmingly on individual experience which has been conditioned by contemporary culture and values. We are troubled by the process that has been used in recent studies on human sexuality within the ELCA. The conversations on this issue thus far have largely focused on personal experience and the sharing of anecdotes, rather than on the teaching of Holy Scripture and the theological and confessional witness of the church. We call the church to recognize that personal experience is not a reliable interpretive key to the Word of God.

4. Three strategies have been proposed by those who wish to change the present policy. One is "ordination to place," in which a non-celibate homosexual is ordained exclusively to serve one congregation. A second is "synodical option," which permits synods to set their own standards in this matter. A third strategy might be termed "conscientious pluralism," in which traditional and revisionist perspectives on these matters are allowed to coexist in the church. Any of these proposals would destroy the unity of the ELCA and of its ordained ministry.

5. We understand the genuine suffering and challenge that our homosexual brothers and sisters face. We repudiate all forms of prejudice and hatred, but we believe that Christian love requires the clear proclamation of God's truth which alone can free and reconcile us. Sensitive pastoral care for homosexual persons will include compassion, encouragement and the same call to repentance and chastity that God continually places before us all.

Because we love the whole church, many of us are facing a potential crisis of conscience regarding the Evangelical Lutheran Church in America. We earnestly desire to remain actively engaged in the life and mission of our church, but we observe that the ELCA is becoming schismatic and sectarian. We therefore pray that our church's reflection on human sexuality be determined by an obedient listening to the Word of God and by a faithful witness to that Word.